This book is the result of collective work and discussion. The ideas developed in it, and their final shaping, owe most to Jean-Michel Baer, Isabelle Bouillot, Yves Chaigneau, Jacques Delors, Jean-Baptiste de Foucauld, Denise Mairey, Jean-Louis Moynot, Jean-Marc Ouazan, Didier Oury, Bertrand Schwartz, Paul Thibaud and Jérôme Vignon.

Our Europe

The Community and
National Development

◆

JACQUES DELORS
and Clisthène

Translated by Brian Pearce

VERSO
London · New York

First published as *La France par L'Europe* by Grasset, Paris 1988
This translation first published by Verso 1992
© Editions Grasset et Fasquelle 1988
Translation © Verso 1992
All rights reserved

Verso
UK: 6 Meard Street, London W1V 3HR
USA: 29 West 35th Street, New York, NY 10001–2291

Verso is the imprint of New Left Books

ISBN 0–86091–380–5

British Library Cataloguing in Publication Data
A catalogue record for this book is available from the British Library

Library of Congress Cataloging in Publication Data
A catalogue record for this book is available from the Library of Congress

Typeset by Goodfellow & Egan Phototypesetting Ltd, Cambridge
Printed in Great Britain by Bookcraft (Bath) Ltd

Contents

Preface to the English Edition

THIS book will soon be four years old. Its aim is both social and political – to set the future of France within the perspective of ever-increasing interdependence on a global scale and, for this reason, to include it in the process of building Europe. The world has changed somewhat since its first publication, but the main trends on which its viewpoint is based have been broadly confirmed.

The European Community itself is a fair way towards passing through further stages on the way to integration: monetary union and a nascent political union. Its authority in world affairs has been substantially strengthened. With aid to Eastern European countries, trade negotiations of major importance with the United States and Japan, economic integration and the search for a common foreign policy, it has become the one and only reference point for the sharing of sovereignty by great nations. This is not happening without some difficulty. Nevertheless, whether or not one likes the options chosen together by the Twelve, this community provides an essential example today, at a time when we are seeing new tensions appearing between nations, peoples and ethnic groups everywhere.

Even more important than the integration and assertion of the Community's role to radically changing worldwide relations have been the upheavals in Eastern Europe.

At first, the effects of perestroika on East–West relations created a mood of optimism. The collapse of the regimes which had been imposed on the countries bordering the Soviet Union, the Soviet–American negotiations and the unification of Germany put an end to the Cold War. Democracy, justice and world peace seemed to be advancing.

However, in the light of the Gulf War, the deadly clashes in Yugoslavia, the abortive coup in Moscow and the destabilizing of the Union of Soviet Republics, we can see how dangerous and difficult the road of world progress is. We can see how very hard it is to go over from the disintegration that is the price of regained freedom to a reintegration based on the values that underlie the actual exercise of freedom and democratic pluralism.

All this, moreover, is happening on a planet where imbalances are getting worse, with worldwide competition and the advance of technology deepening afresh the economic and social inequalities between nations. In other words, the North–South problem is still with us.

Must we, then, consider this book to be out of date? We do not think so. For while it could not foresee a series of bewildering events (which were never on the cards), its investigation is based upon the fundamental trends in the world's development and set in a perspective which none of the events in the recent past has succeeded in invalidating: the perspective of a social democracy which, in the real-life circumstances that must be faced, is inspired by the humane ideals of democratic socialism, stripped of archaisms, errors and illusions. Who, today would presume to overthrow capitalism? But there is no need to glorify uncontrolled 'liberalism', and we can, without excessive statism, develop the association between those who produce their contemporary world and the competitive freedom of entrepreneurs. The place of the individual in society and opportunities for creativity can flourish only the more richly if this is done.

No doubt the authors of *Our Europe* failed to take full account of all problems present and to come, such as the problems of the worldwide growth of immigration. They did, however, warn of the danger to democracy created by the chauvinism and racist manipulation of this reality which play on social anxieties.

Also, no doubt, the serious problems of North–South relations should have been dealt with as a matter of extreme urgency which affects the entire future of humankind. Lacking, too, is an approach to such vital questions as our planet's ecology, disarmament security and peace. 'Clisthène' is only a group of friends who, though both committed and qualified, are few in number and deeply involved in their regular work. And, above all, nobody can aspire to exhaust a subject in a single book.

The chief purpose of this work is to discover the meaning of a history which has now almost been written – that of the opening of France on to the world of today, and that of the relaunching of the European Community in the 1980s, through the hard experience of the French Left in government. The questions discussed – the opening on to the world, Europe, the modernizing of the state and its relations with society, business, education, employment, work and solidarity – are those which confront the political life of every developed country today. When politics – the art of government and the science of the possible – is in crisis in several countries of Western Europe, everyone is called upon to rise to the heights of responsible citizenship and to contribute thereby to the debate and to the construction of a collective venture. Democracy is victorious in the East, and what joy that brings to all of us; but democracy in the West needs invigorating. We are looking to create a true community of responsible men and women, not a collection of individuals shut in on themselves and guided only by their own feelings or their own narrow interests.

British friends who are kind enough to read this book and who are, like the French, properly attached to their own traditions and their own nation, will find echoed in it, we hope, questions that face all the countries of our Europe. How can we remain ourselves in this world and regain an influence in it worthy of Europe's role in history? How – each of us in accordance with his own political inclinations – can we restore soul and content to thought and action in the service of our societies and their betterment?

The reader will soon understand that what has inspired us is a desire to restore breadth of vision to politics, and to strengthen the responsibility of each citizen to see that this is done.

Jacques Delors and Jean-Louis Moynot

ONE

An Opening on to the World

Every economic policy has been tried, and every one has failed, in the last dozen or so years, to have any real effect on the course of events. None of them has turned the tide of unemployment and endowed France with a degree of overall competitiveness that could stand lasting comparison with that of our chief rivals. From those of us who have briefly stood at the helm of France's economy, this might sound like a somewhat masochistic confession but it is simply the recognition of a fact. This applies both to the supporters of Colbert's ideas and to the disciples of Adam Smith: the latter, with the strident zeal typical of neophytes, will not let us forget that it was the former who ruled the roost long before 1981. From pump-priming to austerity, from recovery to severity, the end of the tunnel is like Zeno's arrow, which vibrates, flies, yet does not fly – it is when you think you can see it that it is farthest away. In 1975 or 1981, 1976–8 or 1982–3, everything happened as though those policies affected only the visible tip of the iceberg. Circumstances, the international environment, chance, bad luck, accident or necessity have restricted their effects. We haven't been given enough time, some cry. Indeed? France is not Italy: in our country the stability of

1

institutions is no illusion. So, no doubt, we shall have to find
another way of looking at things and ask different questions.

Conflicting conceptions of France

Everybody knows that France boasts a considerable variety of
cheeses, and almost as great a diversity of conceptions which
struggle in conflict with each other to make their respective marks
on the state machine and the movement of society, in that order.
Despite the current tone of political discourse, influencing the state
machine still seems to be a much more gratifying enterprise than
influencing the movement of society. Perhaps, though, this is an
attitude which has, over the centuries, taken root so deeply in our
collective consciousness that it has become second nature to us.

Look at our liberals, for instance. They deserve respect, living as
they do in a country which has only ever considered the virtues of
the market with suspicion – a country where, traditionally, all
social forces, with the employers in the lead, have ganged up to
restrict its effects. So heavily burdened a past might have induced
modesty and led to a thoroughly pragmatic approach. But no –
France's neo-liberals have run straight into the trap laid for them
by their lack of inspiration. They have overlooked a dimension
which is inherent in every form of economic and social life:
membership of groups, which implies that each individual has
other criteria besides himself. He measures his own situation and
progress not merely by his own personal well-being but also in
relation to the advances or retreats made by the various groups to
which he feels he is linked.

To left-wing thinkers, on the contrary, this concept of group
membership is familiar, even if they use different terms for it.
Membership of a social class has become – outside the realm of
Marxism, which created the concept – a classic way of analysing
and organizing society, used by market specialists and bishops
alike.

The trouble is that membership of a class has long since proved
inadequate for defining *all* the memberships to which a French

citizen can lay claim. The circles in which we have recently come to include ourselves are no longer concentric. They have fragmented into many dimensions, none of which possesses the graceful harmony characteristic of the circle. Unemployment, yes, but also television, fashion, eating habits – even sexual behaviour – have contributed much more to this explosion than politics which, however, is obviously suffering from it.

The limits and weaknesses of these conceptions

This fragmentation of French society into subgroups which live – more or less consciously – as though self-enclosed is probably the most noxious heritage from the traditional and implacable quarrels among our people. In this we perceive traces of many powerful historical currents, from the home-loving France which encourages reactionary attitudes to the France which is still nostalgic for a purifying Stalinism: with, in between, all the various shades of protectionist mercantilism, colonial imperialism and state socialism.

This stratification of apparently closed social groups gives rise to systems which are unaware of each other's existence. It leads to a one-dimensional reading of history which can be aggressive and in any case does not work. Or – to put it more precisely – if it seeks to work, it works exclusively in a reactionary direction. Those same people who, in a certain magazine, do not hesitate to charge the French Revolution with genocide also circulate the familiar doubts about the reality of the gas-chambers and go into raptures over the joys of life in South Africa.

As for the Left, it cannot claim to be totally innocent either. The incantatory chanting about 'the people of the Left' which went on in 1981–2 implied a kind of exclusionism, and the great dispute over the proposed incorporation of Catholic schools into the state system which brought about the downfall of Mauroy's government also resulted from an out-of-date notion of history.

A second disadvantage is that these exclusions deny the existence of deep, ancient and permanent interpenetrations between social groups and between cultures. The resulting models enable one to understand the economy of the ghetto, but not that of exchange and, still less, that of the gift. It is not, of course, a question of moralizing about this situation, but of examining the practical consequences of the present system, and some of the ways in which it could develop. This is all the more necessary because the segmentation of the French into hostile groups causes them to be even more cut off from the world around them than they would be otherwise, so that they take even longer to become aware of the interdependences that actually exist. There is a strong dialectical link between our incapacity to live as a dynamic whole, our domestic tensions, and our difficulty in understanding the outside world. In other words, our system of closed memberships actually seems to be one reason for the economic policy failures mentioned above.

Towards a grouping of open memberships

How can we preserve a personal identity, with all its weight of allusions to a particular history and tradition, a social or family group, without thereby shutting ourselves off from other traditions and other groups? How can we invent – or perhaps reinvent – a system of *open* memberships? This is the issue – apparently both banal and conciliatory, but nevertheless absolutely relevant – involved in a reconstitution of the values around which the French Left defines itself.

Let us take the matter further. Since what is involved is the promotion of a social and political organization made up of open memberships, this issue is not confined to the Left but concerns society as a whole. Internally, an approach of this sort aims at doing away with all forms of exclusion and marginalization: externally, it aims at inserting France, in an active and balanced way, into the world economy.

If we look first at our country's internal situation, we shall get a better idea of how strong these interdependences are.

When, in 1957, beneath a tapestry depicting the fight between

4

the Horatii and the Curiatii, Christian Pineau and Maurice Faure signed the Treaty of Rome for France, they probably had no idea how far the worldwide system of interdependences was going to develop. But they did know that they were initialling the birth certificate of a revolution, because this treaty advocated freedom of circulation for people, goods, services and capital. From the outset, the Community defined itself not as a mere Customs union but as a real centre of economic activity on a global scale, aimed explicitly at contributing to the progress of international trade.

An irreversible opening

An ambition of this kind was not a matter of course for France – just remember the piercing shrieks the employers uttered at that time! . . . But the choice of an opening on to the world was all the more irreversible because, in the same period, the process of decolonization which had begun with the ending of the struggle in Indochina was reaching fruition. Within less that ten years, France ceased to be the metropolis of a colonial empire rich in many protected markets, to become a middle-ranking power burdened with a cumbersome past. As a result, the pressure of external constraints would be felt all the more keenly as the years went by.

In 1981, during the first months of the Left government, there was a very strong urge to reverse this tendency, so burdensome seemed the interdependences which had proliferated along with the increase in commercial exchanges. Faced with the pressure of capital flight, ought one not to challenge the cosmopolitan greed of the multinationals' return to mercantilism, and seek – or rather reconquer – on our national territory the resources needed for technological and industrial recovery on a global scale?

Even if there is such a thing as a creative utopia, this did not deserve such an attractive description. The question is no longer how and to what extent we can break free of external constraint. What matters from now on is recognizing that the solution to our problems is wholly bound up with the variables of interdependence: exchange rates, interest rates, growth in world trade,

TWO

Interdependences

W HAT does interdependence mean? The answer is glaringly obvious. In every country an ever-increasing number of men and women work to satisfy the needs of foreign enterprises and consumers, not those of their fellow-citizens. The growth of world trade surpasses that of world production by one or two points every year. While it is true that the gap between them has tended to narrow in the last twenty years, this has happened only because production itself has been internationalized.

This kind of extraversion is no longer a peculiarity of the European economies, which pioneered it. New regional groupings are being formed: in South-East Asia around Japan: in Latin America around Brazil: while India, Egypt and Nigeria are becoming, in their own ways, centres of economic influence.

The three forces

Economic interdependence is brought about not by a single force, but by three converging and mutually sustaining elements. The most spectacular, and the one with the most immediate and often brutal effects, is financial and monetary. It manifests itself in the globalization of capital which was set in motion some fifteen years ago by the explosion of Eurodollars and later increased almost beyond belief through the proliferation of financial mechanisms and electronic aids. Today it is enough for a few thousand operators to be installed, day and night, at the same 'sign of the green screens' for parallel variations in long-term interest rates to be effected simultaneously in Tokyo, New York and Buenos Aires.

However, complementarity is still the vehicle of inter-dependence. It is sustained by the 'comparative advantages' which have enabled newly industrialized countries rapidly to increase their share in the market for manufactured goods: 10 per cent in 1970, 15 per cent in 1980 and 20 per cent today. What will it be in the year 2000? But the irruption of new technologies and the diversification of needs sharpened by the increase in quaternary services[1] have caused complementarity between the developed economies to revive. Despite the spectacular battles of the 'war of the chips', we see a prodigious increase in trading of high-quality goods within the USA–Japan–Europe triangle. Half of Europe's consumption of electronic goods is already supplied by North American and Japanese producers. But the Japanese market will itself have to open up, and it is estimated that in 1990 American and European goods will account for 20 per cent of Japanese consumption.

Finally, new links of interdependence are being forged by co-operation agreements for the introduction of new technology, the exploitation of patents and the recognition of common systems of technical standards. Japan seems ready to accept the creation of a Euro–Japanese working group with the task of harmonizing standards for high-definition television. This would be both a tribute to the technological capacities of the old continent and a sign of the Japanese manufacturers' unwavering determination to enter the lists in Europe's future markets.

There can, then, be no room for doubt. Even though there are still large commercial regions, the globalization of markets for goods and services is almost complete. It underlies the entire strategy of businesses, which on this basis mobilize international financial and technological resources.

The false debate about protectionism

Is it possible for a nation, or a group of nations, to withdraw from interdependence? We can easily imagine that a government in difficulties, with serious social problems and threatened by domestic pressure, might ask this question, and that is quite legitimate. It gave rise to a debate in France in March 1983 and remains a permanently open question – even more dramatically open, moreover, in Mexico, Brazil, Argentina, Peru and numerous African countries. Yet none of these countries has finally decided not to repay its debts. In 1983 France did not choose to have recourse to protectionist self-enclosure. In all these cases the remedy would have been worse than the disease, because it would have caused an immediate, large-scale recession.

In theory, a group of countries could withdraw from the world game by organizing, say, a debtors' syndicate, but this would not be practicable. Actually, what unites the countries of a given region is less strong than what binds them to the rest of the world. Brazil, for example, will never be able to do without the support of American or Japanese banks.

Go under or manage – the real choice

While it is true that one cannot withdraw from interdependence, it is nevertheless true also that interdependence brings some chaos and disruption in its wake. The world market, short-sighted and incoherent, regulates in its own way – that is, badly – the imbalances which it continually engenders. The 'invisible hand' of the classical economists is certainly very heavy, as we can see if we look at the major 'adjustments' which have been features of the past fifteen years.

In 1973–4 the quadrupling of the price of energy put an end to two decades of excessively unequal exchange between producers of raw materials and producers of manufactured goods. An immense redistribution of income got under way, along with an unprecedented wave of investment in the Third World due to the recycling of petrodollars. Inflation increased rapidly, resulting in 1979 in a spectacular collapse of the international currency, the dollar.

A fresh adjustment took place in 1979–81: this time the creditors got their own back on the debtors. Real interest rates were fixed for a long time at more than 4 per cent – that is to say, well above average expectations of growth. World inflation would be throttled, but another disease would now emerge – the flare-up of indebtedness in a large section of the Third World. From 1986 onwards an additional threat loomed: United States indebtedness. Today, the total Third World debt amounts to approximately twelve hundred billion dollars, while that of the United States, if it continues to grow at the present rate, will reach one thousand billion dollars at the end of the eighties. These two imbalances, which are unsustainable, call for a third adjustment 'imposed by the market'.

Logically, this could amount to a comeback by the debtors. Going from one rescheduling to the next, under the pressure of interest rates out of all proportion to potential income (meaning exports), the capital originally borrowed by some poor countries has already been refunded to their crditors three or four times over. This infernal machine draws interest rates upwards, impelled, somehow, by a feeling that the loans cannot be redeemed. At the same time it strangles the debtors, who are deprived of their ability to equip themselves, to prepare for the future, or even to carry out the essential minimum of social policy. In Africa, debt servicing accounted in 1987 for more than 30 per cent of receipts from exports, in Latin America the corresponding figure was 45 per cent. Worse still, the poor countries have become net exporters of capital, since the banks, now more suspicious than they used to be, have stemmed the flow of private loans. In that same year, 1987, those countries paid back thirty billion dollars more than they received, and it is neither probable nor desirable that poor countries should finance rich countries over the long term.

But history loves surprises, expecially when it is in a caustic mood. The 19th of October 1987, called 'Black Monday' by all the newspapers, did not see the billions of dubious loans made by Western banks go up in smoke, but it did see the dissolution, in a sort of interstellar void, of part of the savings of individuals and enterprises throughout the world. This financial earthquake is an indication of how another adjustment might happen – not through a resurgence of inflation but through a period of economic low water, in the United States as elsewhere, which could bring down high interest rates and reduce America's external deficit, at least for a time, by reducing imports.

Geofinance as Aesopian language

The circumstantial diagnosis is less important, however, than the new mechanisms whose most perverse aspects were highlighted by the stock-market crash. To call it a crash is no exaggeration: 25 per cent in New York, 20 per cent in Tokyo, 35 per cent in London on that notorious Monday: figures not seen since 1929. A few days earlier the average yield from quoted shares in the United States was three points less than that from fixed-income investments. A gap like this would have been unthinkable at any other time, and it would 'normally' have led to rates being adjusted much sooner.

The new financial mechanisms infinitely increase the opportunities for credit, and claim to offer guarantees against risk – on both stock markets and the other financial markets – to operators who do not engage in pure speculation. For a long time they have allowed an expectation of increased rates which bears no relation to the way business incomes and the profits distributed to shareholders have actually evolved. This disparity is merely one symptom of what has been called – for want of a better term – the uncoupling of the real economy from the financial economy. Some figures will serve to illustrate this phenomenon.

Between 1982 and 1986 the gross industrial product of the twenty-four OECD countries increased by no more than 13 per cent.[2] The number of unemployed consequently increased from 21.5 million to 31.3 million. During this period the world index of the financial markets increased by 130 per cent – or ten times more quickly than the real economy.

On the exchange markets, transactions increased exponentially. They reached two hundred billion dollars per day on the three most important markets – or, at the very least, twenty-five times the amount involved in the day-to-day transactions directly connected with world trade. It follows that exchange rates no longer bear any relation to the basic facts of the real economy, such as inflation or the trade balance. Incoherence and volatility prevail more and more in currency fluctuations.

Given these conditions, it is difficult not to establish a connection between certain aspects of this uncoupling – especially the failure to correct imbalances quickly – and the formidable development of the new financial mechanisms – which are meant, partly, to cover the risks linked with changes in exchange rates or interest rates. They thus favour the liquidity or rapidity of transactions and give less and less attention to the quality of the loans themselves. So we see the expansion of markets which are secondary in relation to the primary financial markets in direct touch with the real economy – secondary markets which, in a sense, revolve around themselves.

Lacking a true sense of direction, these secondary markets intensify the vicissitudes of the real economy. One word or phrase more or less correctly interpreted can, like a trail of gunpowder, light up screens all over the world – all the more so because the speed of transactions implies an increasing automation of orders to sell or buy. On 20 October 1987 operators feared both the breakdown of overheated computers and the dense clusters of orders spewed out by stupid and malicious accounting programmes. In the end, the new financial economy, 'geofinance', by intensifying the uncertainties of a world economy which is difficult to interpret, undoubtedly bears some responsibility for the high real rates of interest which are strangling the growth of world trade.

Yet one must be careful not to throw the baby out with the bathwater. Geofinance has its merits. Its development, inseparable from the globalization of markets, is practically irreversible. A prodigious source of innovation, it constantly brings various categories of borrowers and savers the financial products they need. As a creator of real services it is indispensable to the life of industry. Think, for instance, of the role played by stock options in the new ownership schemes, or primary cover for investment risks, or the build-up of commercial or technological co-operation networks. It is important not to attack the wrong issue, out of either mere ignorance or nostalgia for a quantity theory of money which has largely been outgrown (though not replaced). The information, organization, even employment of a new financial system, and an effective and adequate allocation of resources to good debtors – that is the issue before us today.

A balance such as this assumes the existence of rules. In the hope that a minimal level of strictness might return to the most sensitive international markets, that the excesses of automatic procedures might be curbed, and that the scale of some very short-term transactions might be restricted, the operators them-selves are praying for reregulation. At least, there is a feeling that they would not be opposed to it, provided it did not consist exclusively of mechanical and hermetically sealed barriers. In other words, we are waiting for the central bankers, the auth-orized protectors of savers, to lay down a sensible set of rules.

Musgrave's lesson

Since the financial, monetary and commercial markets have demonstrated their short-sightedness, they doubtless need to be provided with a 'government'. And since they have become worldwide, this must be a 'world government'. The first lesson of Black Monday is that, although we did not want it, we have to put up with the consequences.

Put forward baldly like this, the notion of a 'world govern-ment' belongs to the realm of provocative fiction. Let us persist with this provocation for a moment and summon to the rescue the American economist Richard Musgrave, who showed, some twenty-five years ago, that society's well-being depends on the state's capacity to ensure the harmonization of three economic functions: allocation, regulation and distribution means the correcting of those unevennesses which the market cannot iron out.

If the markets which have become worldwide function in so disordered a fashion, this is because interdependences have not been brought under political control. They are increasing at the expense of national mechanisms which are not being replaced. By employing – for the sake of convenience – the quite fictitious notion of 'world government', we can see that such a government would have to undertake Musgrave's three tasks.

The question of regulation is certainly the most urgent. For the moment it is the responsibility of G7, the monetary club made up of the seven countries which consider themselves the most highly industrialized – the United States, Japan, Germany, France, Great Britain and Canada, who meet once a year at the 'summit'. By any practical criteria, the attempts at co-ordination and co-operation made by G7 since 1986[3] have fallen far short of what is needed. Moreover, not all the club's members show the same degree of enthusiasm for renovating the international monetary system. And ought not G7 to go further along the path of globalization by admitting to membership, for example, the more advanced countries of South-East Asia or Latin America?

The task of distribution consists above all in implementing an equitable and lasting method of dealing with the debt problem of the poor countries. The Director-General of the International Monetary Fund (IMF), Michel Camdessus, and his immediate predecessor, Jacques de La Rosière, grappled with the two crucial problems: providing inexpensive means of financing the most critical situations, and devising a clear-cut system, based on conditionality, designed to reward genuine reorganization and modernization efforts.

Finally, the problem of allocation concerns the rules by which the world market functions. The Herculean labours undertaken over decades, in the sphere of trade, through GATT (General Agreement on Tariffs and Trade), must now be continued through the construction of sensible rules to govern financial activities.

It is thus not out of place to contemplate the possibility that mechanisms might be created which would ensure that world markets function coherently and dynamically. Let us agree, once more, that the image of a 'world government' is a caricature and the concept behind it is impracticable. Both, however, would be replaced to advantage by a common political will, among the chief economic powers of both North and South, to apply themselves simultaneously to the main fields – monetary, financial and commercial – in which interdependence prevails.

Predicting Europe

The notion of a common political will is beginning to acquire meaning in our old continent. However, in the face of the Japano–American duopoly, the lack of cohesion among Europeans is still startling.

That global interdependences should be subject year after year, to the hazards of election dates and the state of the dominant economy is nothing new, but is it inevitable? There is only one way to mobilize will against chance: the creation of a power sufficiently credible to be able to fight for the cause of international co-operation. None of the partners of the United States possesses, on its own, the capacity to do that, even if it wished to. But if the nations of Europe were to unite effectively in the key domains of interdependence, they would acquire the necessary power.

Germany alone cannot, in the role of locomotive, supply the dynamism needed to ensure that the inevitable adjustment of America's external deficit will take place without too much damage. A collective initiative for growth – even a modest one – undertaken by all Europeans together would constitute a thoroughly credible answer to this problem.

Similarly, France alone, despite her African links and her senior civil servants' incomparable experience in these matters, lacks the means to galvanize a constructive revival of the debate on indebtedness. But the Twelve, taken together, control 45 per cent of the votes in the governing body of the IMF, and by using these they could un-block the funds so barbarously labelled 'the structural adjustment facility', initiate the creation of new special drawing rights, and lay down practical foundations for a more fruitful conception of conditionality.

In the monetary sphere we can no longer expect the yen alone to form a counterweight to the dollar that would be adequate to stabilize the exchange rate system. Even though we may doubt the purity of their motives, the Japanese do have the right to call on the Europeans to take part in the management of international liquidities. Now the Europeans already have at their disposal the appropriate mechanism – namely, the ECU – and this should be given a political status that would be commensurate with the growing financial and commercial integration of Europe.

From economic interdependence to cultural and political interdependence

The globalization of the economy brings in its wake all sorts of issues which may sometimes be described as bellicose and sometimes as peaceful, but are all fundamentally important. The currents of economic exchange bring with them also the languages, customs and values of those who drive them. We may already have reached the point where economic issues are inseparable from cultural ones. What would happen if Europe's audio-visual products proved incapable of withstanding the commercial pressure of American and Japanese products?

The political issues of defence and security are, *a fortiori*, completely interlocked with economic issues. To mention merely one question that is dominating today's international scene: it appears that awareness of the manifold consequences of this fact is an essential element in the new course taken by the foreign policy of the Soviet Union.

In quite different conditions, France needs to re-evaluate profoundly the issues that face her, so as to work out a strategy for herself which will take into account the growing complexity of global interdependence.

THREE

Europe:
The Dream and
the Difficulty

W HAT is Europe? A grouping that is unique in the density
and quantity of its commercial exchanges, a comparative
oasis of monetary order and even of financial equilibrium, and a
considerable reserve of internal growth. It possesses a demographic, historical and cultural wealth, homogeneous even in its
extreme diversity, which, doubtless, no other region of the world
can claim. To be sure – and we shall come back to this in a moment
– external challenges often find the Europeans divided. If we take a
close look at these challenges, though, we see that, on the
contrary, they actually bring to the fore Europe's common
features. The very term 'Community' which is used for the
countries which signed the Treaty of Rome could have no better
application. Do not the Six of yesterday and the Twelve of today
recognize in one another the same essential principles – democracy,
human rights, self-determination of nations? Do they not share the
same concern for world equilibrium?

Today democracy prevails right across Europe, and in this privi-
leged situation we must not underestimate the force of attraction
exercised by the European Community, nor the guarantee it
provides against any adventure in the opposite direction. The

17

Spaniards and the Portuguese are well aware of that. But every European understands, too, the fragility of democracy, the threat to it posed by enemies who speculate on its moral principles in order to weaken it, since, by definition, the democratic end does not justify every means.

Democracy, balance between state and society, between the collective and the individual, is Europe's model. This fundamental law, which unites us all, must be the object of all our vigilance. Together, we are the stronger for exercising it. This question has always preoccupied those workers for Europe who have operated away from the halls of power and the platforms. 'The beginning of Europe', said Jean Monnet, 'was a political vision, but even more was it a moral one. Europeans had gradually lost the capacity to live together and combine their creative power, their contribution to progress. Their role in the civilization they had themselves created seemed to be declining.' The division of Europe into East and West, the fact that some European peoples had been deprived of the right to put into practice the political values they share with us – values acquired through a common history – bears witness to this loss. Can this, at last, give rise to a common awareness?

The threat has not vanished. Will our political stability, the model of our society, resist if our countries let themselves go on sliding down the slope of decline? Especially as this downward slide is beginning to show itself in our inability to respond to the demographic challenge which can be summed up in two figures. In 1983 the Europe of the Ten included 5.8 per cent of the world's population. In 2020, according to the projections made by the INED (National Institute of Demographic Studies) it will include no more than 3.3 per cent. France is not so badly placed as some in this connection, since her fertility rate of growth exceeds 1.8 per cent, whereas in the Northern countries, notably Germany, it is only 1.5 per cent. (The fertility rate needed to maintain population is 2.1 per cent.) A prolongation of the demographic deficit would have serious consequences – not only because it might induce a certain *fin-de-siècle* slackness, but also because it would entail increased dependence by the non-active on the active section of the population (and, unless there is a radical reform of their basis, collapse of the welfare systems, whose current financial difficulties are merely forewarnings) and a marked imbalance of population between the two shores of the Mediterranean.

Let us conclude this brief digression about the future and take a look at the Europe of today, because the threat is here already. Although Europe still ranks among the principal economic and military groupings, it seems more often to be the object of contradictory ambitions, strategic conflicts or trade rivalries than the expression of a conscious will. Hence this vague, uneasy feeling we have, during crises and even in periods of calm, that the fate of Europe, of the countries that make up Europe, is being determined independently of Europe.

Between the Yom Kippur War and the emergence of a religious fundamentalism which has risen up against a misrepresented Europeanism, between the Soviet expansionism of the 1970s and the resurgence of conservative America, between the threats of bankruptcy by the poor countries and South-East Asia's entry on to the world economic scene, the initiative has slipped from our grasp, although we have suffered the full effects of these events. Faced with the important changes observable in the Soviet Union and the initiatives of Mikhail Gorbachev, Europe is still hesitant and its opinions are divided. A first step has been taken with the statement of mutual recognition by Comecon and the Community, followed by the establishment of diplomatic relations with five countries of Eastern Europe. A second step has begun with the Council of Ministers' decision to entrust to the Commission the task of exploring the possible content of an agreement with the USSR. But we are far from united in our views on the questions raised by this new deal. What are the Soviet leader's aims? Are we, as some say, about to make some ill-considered concessions? Is America about to uncouple itself from Europe? Or do these changes, on the contrary, offer new opportunities to Europe? On all these levels, though they correspond to chapters in its ongoing history, Europe is too often merely a spectator of a play in which it is itself the principal and immediate theme.

True, none of the countries of the Community has abandoned its role in the world, the maintenance of its rank among the nations, and that is a good thing. But what is this rank? Whether economic or geopolitical, Europe's real successes have hitherto been inconceivable without the presence of the American umbrella. The sphere in which our countries can manoeuvre is narrowing. Our economies bow before the law, the currency, of the dominant power. After the 'thirty glorious years', after three decades of a growth thanks to which we thought we were recovering strength and authority, we have to admit, bitterly but clear-sightedly, that our efforts have been inadequate. Economic growth was indispensable, that is obvious, but it was not all that was needed. The ambitions of each country remained confined in mediocrity because the group as a whole proved unable to define a common destiny.

If reactions within the Community had been violently different, we could have offered another diagnosis. But the similarity of developments is striking, whether we look at the nature of social organization, the degree of economic interdependence or the nature of the difficulties encountered. As a result of the oil shocks, which were detonators rather than causes of our problems, Europeans were faced, if they were to make the necessary adjustments, with a choice between three solutions. The crudest of these would have been a retreat into protectionism. This they fortunately rejected. Such a cosy response, an aseptic enclosure which isolates the sick person, lengthens convalescence, makes re-education more painful, and is the very negation of the Community spirit. Besides, it is not only the health of our own countries that is at stake. Many young nations set their economic and also their political hopes on the development of their relations with Europe. That implies greater access to our markets. Barring their exports of agricultural produce or manufactured goods would mean, for them, more far-reaching consequences than an immediate loss of expected income. Already in that period Europe was trying to promote an original and more balanced relationship with the South, codified by the Lomé agreements. This entire approach would have been brought into question and, furthermore, Europe's own values would have suffered.

A second solution would have taken the form of a sharp

alignment of our production costs with those of our competitors. This would have meant a 30 per cent reduction in Europe's total income, a figure which is enough by itself to show that it was unthinkable, given the European model – not to mention the fact that it would have entailed a sharp reduction in imports from the Third World, due to the fall in purchasing power.

The remaining solution, then, was to increase the efficiency of the productive apparatus. The European countries applied themselves to this task and registered advances in productivity that were higher than those achieved by the United States or even, in certain sectors, by Japan. The speeding-up of the substitution of capital for labour has been accompanied, however, by a heavy cost in unemployment, some of whose victims have been better compensated than others. While the rising tide of unemployment seems today to have been better contained, it nevertheless remains at an intolerably high level. The shortage of jobs is still the major failing in our common model, even though there are substantial differences between the member countries. Those with a more progressive system of social relations, education and training have enjoyed better success.

The effects of the crisis have not ceased to make themselves felt. The European process of adjustment is not yet complete. Yet this period has taught us a really remarkable lesson. There has been an end to 'everyone for himself', an attitude which sometimes led to the worst of political solutions. Though severely shaken for more than a decade, the countries of the Community have strengthened their economic cohesion and their democratic infrastructures.

However, Europeans do not seem to be fully aware of this interdependence, this common destiny. Everything happens as though the adventure of the Treaty of Rome (to which most history books do justice, so far, only in a few lines) had developed alongside them, but they had taken no more than a polite interest in it. And so we are not deriving from it all the potential benefits, either economic or political. Is there any other way of acting, though, if we are to recover the initiative, to defend and extend the influence of our common values, than rallying our forces together?

Leading Europe means trying to synthesize the many and

21

sometimes contradictory interests of the member nations, their different conceptions of Europe's identity and future. Common sense tells us that we cannot change in a few years the courses taken by nations which have existed for centuries. The Community is thirty years old, but France is a thousand years old. All the same, there is something simplistic in such a comparison. The European project cannot replace the national project. 'France is our country, Europe our future,' says François Mitterrand. How can we expect nations which, more often than not, have built themselves in conflict one with another, have sought to rule the world, to merge suddenly in one idyllic unity? But perhaps it is this very history full of conflicts that will have its logical outcome in a form of unity? Does not the repetition of European wars, century after century, prove, in the end, that Europe cannot be the seat of an empire, that none of its nations can dominate the others, that they must learn to live together? Does it not mean, now that all the countries of Europe have given up mourning their imperial ambitions, that there must be common acceptance of the need to define a common order?

Once this awareness was achieved, the construction of Europe has, paradoxically, taken the path of 'economic gradualism'. It was not for any lack, in the postwar years, of an effervescence of concepts and repeated calls for the building of a *political* Europe. 'We need institutions set up by the direct vote of Europe's citizens and possessing, in the spheres of economics and defence, that share of sovereignty which will be delegated to them by the participating states.' This was how General de Gaulle criticized the Council of Europe's lack of power in August 1950. All the major actors in the last world conflict and the postwar period advocated political union, either partial or more ambitious. Forty years later, the verdict belongs to history. Economic gradualism (European Coal and Steel Community, European Economic Community) has won the day over the political idea. The institutions set up in order to ensure economic integration are functioning, whatever one may think of how well they function. The institutions intended to create political or military union have failed or, at any rate, have not justified the hopes of those who conceived them.

So, then, it is the economic approach that has ensured the permanence of the European movement, regardless of political hazards and international tempests. Year by year, a foundation has been laid down upon which 'political co-operation' has succeeded in developing. Henceforth this is an integral part of the Treaty of Rome through the implementation of the Single European Act, which aims at the formulation and application of a homogeneous foreign policy for the twelve member countries of the European Community. Although this movement has continued, however, it has only intermittently shown the strength needed if Europe is to speak with one voice. Too often, Europe has hung about arguing on the station platform while history's trains have departed.

Speeding up the European movement, guiding it so that it may contribute to the return of prosperity and employment, working so that our wills may combine and make possible the political expression of Europe – this is the task that faces us today. There have been lost generations, generations whose cowardice brought on disasters, 'spiv generations' that were disillusioned or, rather, disorientated. Today's generations, both adults and adolescents, have both an immense responsibility and an extraordinary opportunity. They will be judged by their capacity to unite Europe in a common aim, to face their common destiny. This ambition calls for politicians possessed of both courage and readiness for self-sacrifice. To please or to build: the choice must be made. To please – meaning to surrender oneself to the joys of 'Europe in words' – or to build – meaning to watch unceasingly, to react to every initiative, to respond to every event which could weaken Europe, divide it or lower its standing in the world.

And this is not a matter only for Europeans. We bear a responsibility towards the young nations which see in our old countries a source of equilibrium, a community with which their relations are based on reciprocal openness. We bear a responsibility also towards the countries of the East with which we are linked by so many cultural ties, and to which we must say that *we* do not hold the monopoly of Europe.

The current crisis is indeed a crisis of confidence and identity. If

FOUR

A New Departure

1992: The necessary objective

JANUARY 1985: Jacques Delors is preparing his 'investiture' speech to the Strasbourg Parliament. The heart of this speech is a plan for achieving a common internal market – that is to say, abolishing administrative and fiscal Customs barriers between member countries of the Community. And, along with this, a date for the completion of that task – a date which, as the months went by, would come increasingly to symbolize it: 1992.

Why this objective, and why this date? The Community had just passed through a period of gloomy stagnation, marked by disputes over the budget and rigid attitudes on the part of the British. To begin with, the virtues of economic integration were becoming blurred. This was shown by the stabilization of commercial exchanges among the Ten in the previous decade. It was therefore important to advance to a new stage of integration. Then, everyone felt that Europe was making too few decisions, and making them wrongly, and that the decision process would become still more difficult with the entry of Spain and Portugal into the Community. In short, Europe was marking time.

Convinced of the need for a fresh start, Jacques Delors systematically explored the possible agents for this. The institutional
question? By attacking this head on he might win over the
Parliament, but would risk reviving ideological debates and causing additional obstacles to emerge. The European monetary
system, one of the few but undeniable successes of the preceding
period? This was not a good moment to give that a new
dimension. The governors of the central banks had just rejected
even a modest set of technical improvements. The Germans, who
wanted to give priority to promoting the liberation of capital
movements, would object vigorously to a proposal that implied a
further step towards a common currency. European defence, then?
Not only were minds not ready for this, but the subject was *ultra
vires* for the European executive.

There remained, as a sort of return to the beginning of the
process, the economic path – the creation of a great common
market, a source of growth and jobs. And since he was going back
to origins, Jacques Delors drew inspiration from the best of them.
Following the example of Jean Monnet, the idea must be turned
into an objective, and that in time must be made concrete by
setting a date – hence 1992. Eight years, the length of two
Commission mandates, would not be too long for realizing such
an ambition. The first Commission would have the task of making
the movement irreversible: the second would complete it. Besides,
fixing a definite date would be the best way to obtain a solemn
commitment from the governments of the member states.

On 14 January 1985 the new chairman made his speech to the
European Parliament and won a big majority. Two months later
the communiqué of the Council of Heads of State and Government, in Brussels, made 1992 official. The movement had been
started – at the very moment when, at last, the difficult negotiations on the admission of Spain and Portugal were brought to a
successful conclusion.

In June another Council of Europe, assembled in Milan,
approved the White Book in which the European Commission set
out the measures to be taken in order to ensure abolition, between
then and 1992, of the physical, technical and fiscal barriers between

the member countries. This Council also decided to hold an inter
governmental conference with the task of preparing the reform of
the Treaty of Rome which would be necessary if the new
objectives adopted by the Community were to be realized. It was
in December 1985 that the Council of Europe discussed and
adopted, in Luxembourg, the texts proposed by the Commission.
This was how the Single European Act came into being. It was an
institutional reform that sought to make the Community's
decision-making process both more efficient and more democratic,
to bring about abolition of internal frontiers, to put into effect
accompanying policies in the social and technological spheres, and
to strengthen the economic and social cohesion of Europe.

More than a year passed before these documents, which opened
the way to a new future, were ratified by the peoples of Europe –
directly through referenda in Denmark and the Irish Republic,
indirectly by the Parliaments of the other member countries. They
still had to be given content, and intentions and actions had to be
brought into conformity. To proclaim a common economic area,
to appeal for its cohesion and balanced development and for
scientific and technological co-operation, is one thing; to put these
principles and plans into practice is another, calling for additional
financial resources to be made available for Europe.

In the absence of such an effort, the European Commission was
convinced that the great market would not come about. There
would, perhaps, be a vague and incomplete free-trade zone
between several Community countries, but this would be reconsidered as soon as an imbalance appeared to which the institutions
would lack the means of reacting. It would be nothing like the
project for a great economic and social grouping, organized,
united, conscious of its strength and responsibilities – that is to say,
capable of showing initiative and reacting in the common interest
of the twelve member countries.

While the Council of Ministers was adopting the first texts, the
European Commission proposed, in February 1987, the 'Delors
package', a co-ordinated set of measures aimed at 'ensuring success
for the Single European Act'. To succeed, however, it was
necessary to reassure and convince. In the first place, the countries

to which the Common Agricultural Policy was dear had to be assured that this policy would not be sacrificed on the altar of the great market of industry and services. Now, this policy was the target of very vigorous attacks, owing to the burden it constituted on the Community's finances (two–thirds of the budget) and the increased expenditure it entailed. Proceeding in the same direction, at the same rate, would have led eventually to condemnation of the agricultural policy. What the Commission proposed was to redefine this policy in the light of the new world deal, and to control expenditure on agriculture (which did not mean reducing it) while guaranteeing a future for the farmers. The Commission's proposal may be summarized as follows: adapt production to demand, give help and support to family farms, take action for rural development, and maintain a firm common position on the international scene in order to get Europe's chief competitors to make the same effort to adjust.

It was also necessary to give assurance to those countries where certain regions were suffering from a delay in development. In this connection, policies had to be adopted, accompanying the creation of the common market, which would help these countries to adapt themselves, to develop their infrastructures, but also to mould their human resources. In this way they would avoid becoming the object of a sort of neo-colonialism on the part of the richer countries. Apart from considerations of ethics and democracy, has not history taught us that attempts at union have often failed because of a will to dominate, whether openly expressed or not, on the protagonist's part? To this end, the 'Delors package' proposed that the means assigned to what are called the structural funds devoted to regional development, social provisions and the direction of agricultural production should be doubled. There were three funds for five objectives: development of backward regions, regeneration of regions suffering from industrial decline, struggle against long-term unemployment, initiating young people into trades, and rural development. Realization of these five objectives would bring about the economic and social cohesion of a Europe without frontiers. The sums devoted to the first of these objectives were comparable to those mobilized by the Marshall Plan.

It was also necessary to convince the Twelve that they were engaged in an undertaking without precedent. So that each member should contribute to the common task according to its means, the 'Delors package' included a reform of the way the Community was financed which made the payments to be contributed by the member countries proportional to each country's relative prosperity. The pledge given in the Single European Act would benefit all the members only if its provisions were carried out in a determined and united way. The ambitions embodied in the project required that, from the outset, all should agree on the aim, and should go forward inspired with the same zeal. The new 'Community Europe', endowed with an innovative fundamental law, had, indeed, an appointment with itself – yet three 'summits' of heads of state and government were needed to ensure that this appointment was not missed.

In Brussels in June 1987 eleven countries gave their approval to the main outlines of the Delors plan. In Copenhagen in December of that same year Europe, poised between resignation and hope, was unable to offer the world anything but a spectacle of division and impotence, two days before the summit at which Reagan and Gorbachev met to sign a disarmament treaty. Then came Brussels – a summit which, though laborious, was eventually crowned with success.

By February 1988, then, the European Community had embraced its new dimension. By rejecting the twelve fold imbalance and dispersion which would have been caused by an uncontrolled diversity, and by giving themselves the means required by the Single European Act, the heads of state and government sealed a 'new Community contract'. The original pact which founded the six-member Community – and was completed, amended and sometimes got round by the successive additions to membership and by events in Europe – now exists in a new form, impelled by new ambitions.

Pragmatic Europe

By a reversal of history, the economic and social forces which the signing of the Treaty of Rome – an eminently political act – had offended the most are now the staunchest supporters of the single market and the co-operation it engenders. They quickly became the ones to take over the task of promoting this huge ambition. At the same time, certain politicians opposed enlargement of the Community (without going so far as to challenge it once it had taken place) or applied themselves to restricting the effect of the Single European Act.

A measure of agreement has been established between Europe's business leaders and trade-union chiefs, though this is still somewhat fragile and ambiguous. The actors on the socioeconomic stage, in taking this step, with all the risks it involves – for the trade unions especially – have certainly been inspired by long-term considerations. Noisy, spectacular mobilizations end in lamentable collapse, it is the more discreet and dynamic ones that bring about salutary changes, such as those changes we are living through now. Getting to grips with the challenges of competitiveness and employment, and subject to the constraints imposed by monetary instability and the excessively high level of interest rates, the social partners now understand that they must seek the means of coping with these difficulties within a European framework.

Europe did not create these problems, nor does it offer any miracle-cure for them. What it does offer is a new dimension, a fresh opportunity for everyone's activity. A market of 320 million people will provide Europe's enterprises with outlets comparable or even superior to those enjoyed by their Japanese and American competitors. At the present time our enterprises confront, on their own continent, markets that are segmented, fractured and protected. To use a sporting metaphor, they have to run 110 metres over the hurdles while their rivals run 100 metres on the flat.

Different technical standards, protectionist health regulations, closed public-service markets, compartmentalized financial services, fiscal and administrative obstacles all combine to hinder Europe's economic life and impede co-operation between Europeans for common purposes. All this is very costly. To gauge the costs more precisely, the European Commission asked a group of independent economic experts from among the most distinguished in Europe to study the subject. On the macro economic plane, this study[1] showed that the abolition of all obstacles to exchange and economic co-operation within the Community would have a strong, positive effect on all economic indicators within ten years. The growth rate of the Community's Gross National Product (GNP) would increase by 4.5 per cent, prices would fall relatively by 6.1 per cent, nearly two million extra jobs would be created, and public and external deficits would be reduced. The study also taught us that if the governments of Europe were to agree to unite their efforts in the sphere of economic policy – that is, to exploit together the areas opened up in this way – the results would be even more remarkable, and would be attained without interfering with control of inflation or internal and external balances. In this scenario, GNP growth rate would increase by 7 per cent and five million extra jobs would be created. These, of course, were mid-term results and potentialities.

Besides their encouraging message, the results of the study also serve as a guide for 'putting together' the great market. Achieving it will be easier the greater the involvement of the member states, their will to co-operate, becomes. On the other hand, if this co-operation proves inadequate, growth in Europe may turn out to be insufficient to mitigate the shocks caused in some spheres by the construction of the great market, and then the process will be in danger of slowing down. The measures decided on by the Brussels meeting of the Council of Europe, favouring cohesion of the European group, provide, in this connection, a structural contribution. They do not relieve governments of the need to learn the lessons of interdependence as these relate to practical policy.

The advantages of the single market may be perceived more realistically from the micro-economic angle; this evaluates the benefits to be expected from the implementation of each of the major measures included in the European Commision's White Book.

The study also shows that the single market will turn out to be a substantial source of economies of scale. Rationalization of production structures in the European arena will enable about a third of industry to reduce its costs by between 1 and 7 per cent, depending on the sector. Overall, the economies of scale would be in the order of 2 per cent of the Community's gross industrial product. Other advantages, too, will result from the increased pressure of competition on overheads, labour allocation and stock management.

At this point one cannot but think of the many administrative headaches we have all suffered when crossing some frontier in Europe – the time wasted, the losses incurred in changing from one currency to another. There was an article in *Newsweek* by an American woman journalist who hid in the cabin of a trailer carrying pears from Antwerp, in Belgium, to Alessandria, in Italy. The average speed of the journey was 20 kilometres an hour (by motorway), owing to the numerous checkpoints, together with the time spent filling in documents and transferring the whole load on to another lorry when they reached Italy – as if a lorry which had crossed Belgium and France without doing any harm might suddenly become a danger to traffic in Italy! Such examples are legion, proving how true it is that defence of national interests makes administrators' imaginations run riot.

Although it is now well known, 'Objective 92' worries people. A panacea for some, a pretext or a threat for others, it gives rise to many questions concerning business's ability to adapt to new conditions of competition and their readiness to launch into new forms of co-operation. What are the implications for their competitiveness, and for the training of their workers? Actually, one can answer these doubts only by confronting them with the opposite kind of doubt, which is much more serious. What will 'non-Europe' bring us? From what will it protect us? What prospects does it open up for us? Has it enabled us to develop a powerful industrial apparatus capable of resisting aggressive competition from the rest of the world? For France, the answer is only too clear. Our trade deficit is chronic, our trading activities are badly targeted. Some large-scale projects that we were so proud of in the 1960s have hung fire. Exchange control has not prevented successive devaluations. And what weight has the franc, on its own, faced with the fluctuations of the dollar? In international trade negotiations, how much power has France in relation to the United States?

Creating Europe means, given the present balance of forces in the world, acquiring a capacity for independent decision-making. Creating Europe means recovering the degree of freedom needed for 'a certain idea of France' – on condition, that is, that we do not daydream. If we are to prepare the future effectively, we must reduce uncertainty. That is why 'Objective 92' ought to serve as the opportunity to revive French planning. The Tenth Plan (1988–92), linking state and regions, social partners, industry and research, is an instrument sufficient to prepare France for this extremely important moment. This plan could analyse the conditions and potential effects of the great market, assess the issues and suggest answers. It would thus participate in mobilizing all economic and social forces, from small and medium sized enterprises to the large-scale ones, from schools to universities, from trade associations to trade unions. If the Twelve are to succeed, each national community must mobilize itself.

FIVE

A Community to be Built

B Y THE sequence of events it initiates and the reactions it stimulates – indeed, by its very logic – a shared economic space engenders a profoundly transformative force for integration. Its effects are not confined to the economic sphere; they reach beyond, to ensure the formation of a social entity in which Europeans will weave a network of fruitful relationships. From now on, the task of everyone with responsibilities in both public and private sphere is to organize this entity and give it life.

The building of the Community calls for three principal kinds of initiative:

- encouraging mobility and co-operation, especially in education, technology and culture;
- anticipating its social, monetary and international implications;
- evolution of the process of change in Europe's institutions.

The links forged between Europeans will develop along with the new freedoms of circulation and settlement, which imply, in particular, that qualifications will be valid throughout Europe.

The success of the inter-university co-operation programmes

launched by the Commission augurs well for this movement, which will enable young people to make themselves available for employment anywhere in Europe and reach consensus on pan-European education and training.

Hardly were COMETT (which enables students to spend a probationary period working in an enterprise in another member country) and ERASMUS (which enables them to pursue part of their studies in a university in another member country) set in motion than hundreds of European universities formed links, establishing common study programmes, exchanging staff, welcoming students from other countries and introducing reciprocal recognition of degrees.

This movement can only become more widespread. It is a pity that some liberal governments have reduced the funds available, though even if these had remained at their initial level they would not have been enough to meet demand, so great is the thirst for co-operation among Europe's universities.

This desire to co-operate is also obvious in science and technology. Besides those brilliant symbols of European know-how Airbus and Ariane, several thousand projects in which business is associated with research centres and universities are now being put into effect within the framework of the Community programmes (ESPRIT, RACE, BRITE) or EUREKA. Whether the task is organizing a more rational allocation of resources, movement in a somewhat enormous market, or assembling the capital needed for under-taking a new technological adventure, the only answer is a Europe-wide answer. The entrance ticket to the world technological contest is expensive, and operators who can expect to enter the fray on their own are increasingly rare. Consequently, the development of the new generation of public telecommunications, now being commercialized, requires a minimum investment of seven billion francs, from which a reasonable profit may be expected only if the sales prospects are fourteen times greater. It would be hard to find an enterprise ready to risk such an operation, given the limited size of the present market, but it would become viable with a more extensive association of enterprises and a wider framework which ensured that markets were commensurate with investments.

The most powerful micro-processor in the world has been created as a result of Franco-British co-operation. More than ten thousand researchers and businessmen are taking part in the European Commission's programmes on information technology. The EUREKA programme launched by François Mitterrand is also enjoying huge success.

Are not the principles of mobility and co-operation at the heart of the European ethos? Let us remember the fantastic mobility of the intellectuals, the thinkers, in medieval Europe; the creation of the first universities; the permission to teach anywhere in Christendom that was granted to graduates from Paris.

The fact that education and culture do not figure in the Treaty of Rome or in the Single European Act, and therefore do not fall within the competence of the Community's institutions, has fortunately not prevented initiatives by intellectuals, authors and artists for the defence and diffusion of European creative work and the values intrinsic to our culture. Nevertheless, it is the case that the Community's potential in this sphere has been only partly exploited. The legal question is not the only obstacle: a certain short-sightedness, a real provincialism, cause cultural policy to amount sometimes merely to the preservation of the circumscribed field. Audiovisual products are a perfect example. Audiovisual productions do not circulate in Europe – or rather, the only ones that do are American; so the shared space exists only for the benefit of extra-European productions. This is paradoxical when we know that a large audience is a precondition for success. Unless Europe responds, film and television production is likely to become less and less accessible to our producers and artists.

The developments of the single market will lead the Europeans to organize in three areas simultaneously: currency, the social sphere, and a common foreign policy. These areas already share 'history', and there are already shared mechanisms and arrangements. But a shared space will entail stronger demands, to which more precise responses will be required.

This is so with the currency question. A European currency is integral to the genetic make-up of the single market. The proliferation of industrial and commercial relations, the constitution of a common financial space, the free establishment of banks and financial intermediaries, all call for a simplification of the mechanisms. How long will it be before a European currency sees the light of day? What form will it take? Proposals are now appearing that would have been unimaginable a few years ago.

There is a suggestion that a European monetary fund should be created: a central European bank. The tide of events is carrying us in that direction, to be sure, but in so delicate a matter progress must proceed one step at a time. Since 1985 Europe's monetary system has twice been strengthened. The currencies that constitute it have thus undergone the radical turbulence connected with the dollar's erratic fluctuations without suffering too much harm. This system must now be extended to those currencies which do not yet participate in it. Utilization of the ECU is being extended to a larger proportion of commercial and financial transactions. A proper money market for the ECU must be established. The European fund for monetary co-operation must be strengthened and given power to intervene in the exchange markets. The central bank and the European currency will follow from these developments.

For this currency, as for the economy as a whole, creation of a shared space ought not to increase European exposure to external pressures. Its purpose is not to open up our markets to the greed of outsiders. The cohesion of the European entity must assert itself against all competitors, so the Community must possess the means of defending its rights, and demonstrate its will to utilize them effectively.

Is this a protectionist reflex? Certainly not. It will be the principles of equity and reciprocity that will dictate the attitude of the European Community when it defines the 'external panel' of the single market. For example, the right to benefit from the opening of the public markets or from free bank loans will be granted only to operators from other countries that offer the same conditions of access to operators from the European Community.

Another organization that is both desirable and necessary is one that would deal with the social domain. All the effort deployed to bring about European recovery across our shared space must contribute towards improving the living and working conditions enjoyed by Europeans. It would make no sense if competition were to develop at the expense of the social protection and working conditions which are the basis of the European model. Europe will not be created if the workers do not feel involved in it, and if it does not have social progress as its ultimate aim.

The task is a difficult one to accomplish in this heterogeneous grouping, where differences in living standards and protection will continue to be very marked for a long time. People must accept that what in their country is not a perceptible improvement in a contract of employment or working conditions may represent real progress somewhere else. Minimum provisions laid down for everyone do not constitute an obstacle to the maintenance and strengthening of more favourable provisions where these exist. This means that in the process of bringing employment conditions into line, together with training and employee representation, improvement of the higher social standards remains possible and desirable, and these standards are objectives for those countries which have fewer advantages at present.

Such are the principles of the Treaty of Rome, and of the Single European Act. But the movement that will bring everyone closer together will not gather momentum until the social partners come into the field. This was why Jacques Delors summoned European employers' and trade-union leaders to Val Duchesse, near Brussels, in January 1985, and urged them to begin a real social dialogue on a Community scale.

For the first time in the history of the Community the social partners adopted, in 1986 and 1987, two 'common opinions' intended to influence negotiations in the member countries. One supports the initiative for growth recommended by the European Commission (strengthened co-operation between states in matters of economic policy). The other concerns provision of information, training and worker participation when new technologies are introduced. New proposals were put forward at the congress of the European Confederation of Trade Unions. Construction of the social space has been on the agenda for the last ten years.

Strengthening the ties between Europeans, jointly attacking major questions of common interest, leads us to consider the competence and functioning of the Community's present institutions. Are these institutions – conceived, as they were, for administering a six-member Community, and reformed in order to achieve the single market – appropriate to the needs and demands of the new shared space?

It would be a mistake to think that an unrestricted Europe, endowed with new objectives and increasing resources, would have no further problems.

If the deregulating freedom of frontier abolition is not to have disappointing consequences, it will be necessary to take firmer measures to bring about a genuine European policy. If the institutional problem has so far been dodged, this was owing to fear of reviving the latent conflict between federalists and confederalists, between partisans and adversaries of the withering-away of the nation-state. To overcome this dilemma it will probably be necessary to circumscribe the European dimension of policy clearly, presenting Europe as a new consideration which will have to be integrated by member states, so that these states, though not dissolved, have their responsibilities defined anew. We shall doubtless have to distinguish between what, perhaps, may be rendered common and entrusted to the people of Europe as a whole, because there is a real convergence of wills and interests (respect for democratic principles, for instance) and what belongs to the sphere of common policies based on negotiation between states (within the Community framework). In any case, the European edifice demands a new architecture. If it is to progress, it must clarify its political concepts.

SIX

The French in Dire Need of the State

I N THEIR haunting sense of decline, the French are concerned not so much with their demographic situation or their adverse economic indicators (a sort of resignation to the existence of unemployment has eventually set in) as with their country's new permeability to foreign infleunces. Having been able until recently to assimilate those who have come to settle in France, because they were sure of controlling their own space both politically and economically, the French looked out on the rest of the world as though from a stronghold. Even in their worst moments, consciousness of unshakeable identity reassured them. Today, however, globalization disturbs the French more than it disturbs their neighbours, who are more used to trading, emigrating, participating in supranational or federal groupings, and defining themselves flexibly in a delicate situation, surrounded by others. The influx of languages, products, customs – even attitudes of mind – from elsewhere has caused them distress. The obsessive assertion of 'Frenchness' on the extreme Right of our political spectrum expresses this new vulnerability, but the panicky chauvinism of Jean-Marie Le Pen would not have gained so much support if the feeling of being caught in a heterogeneous globalization was not aggravated by doubt about the nation's ability to face up to it in a coherent and organized way. In short, the French no longer have confidence in their state.

The estrangement between civil society and the state in France, which harms the one no less than the other, had its immediate origin in the turn taken by Socialist policy in 1983. Since 1981 governing had meant distributing, with the state responding to social demand. External constraint put an end to that generous idyll in which society received, as its due, protection and satisfaction. For lack of agreement, however, no new idea appeared to replace that delusive dream. The policy of 'rigour' failed to signal new reforms inspired by a more active conception of society, remaining, instead, content to silence social considerations in the face of urgent economic exigencies. This meant war, with business representing the front and the rest of society the rear, which had only to tighten its belt and pray for the fighters on whom the nation's salvation depended. Under these conditions the state's role was greatly reduced. And if a regrettable accident of history impelled the state to the forefront once more, it appeared in the cast-off clothing of the Evil One. . . . To a certain extent this socialism without social vision presaged the disconnected, liberal, technocratic state which was to follow – a state fundamentally, even absurdly, pessimistic regarding French society; a state for which any collective value, any sense of solidarity, was to be combated in the name of a mythical tranparency of society to the laws of the economy.

This crisis was extremely serious because it reflected not so much the attitude of our rules as the exhaustion of a centuries-old model, that of the state guiding the nation. If we are to understand the present situation, we must take account of our nation's historical dependence on its state, even though the nation created that state; and recognize, moreover, that there was nothing wrong with that. Right down to our own time it has been under the aegis of a state whose moral superiority and cultural leadership were appreciated that we have enjoyed the most creative eras of our history (the other side of the coin being the fact that failure on the state's part explains our less glorious moments). Through a sort of pernicious trendiness, however, it is currently fashionable to deprecate the French model altogether and hold up other political cultures for our admiration (those of Germany, Sweden, Italy, Japan or the United States, depending on the vagaries of taste and time), cultures which their distinctive features render non-transferable. Rejection of our own tradition and lack of serious reflection on a contemporary history which has nevertheless been lived through most passionately are among the predominant factors in the stalemate suffered by France, especially where the crucial matter of linking the state with civil society is concerned. Consequently, in order to be able to perceive a new role for the state in France, we must begin by thoroughly examining the republican model.

The republican model

Though it is a commonplace, it is useful to remember that our political culture bears the imprint of the 1789 Revolution. France is the country which raised the question of a secular and voluntary basis for government, with no concession and no backsliding, before every other modern state. King Charles I of England had his head cut off because he had encroached upon the traditional liberties of his people; Louis XVI lost his head merely because he was King. The French Revolution was not only a reaction by the social body against the established authority, it laid new foundations for authority. And it is futile, despite some current fashions, to try to reduce this radical character of our revolution to an aberration. On the contrary, it heralded the arrival of all the modern democracies. The only difference was that the French declared, straight out, that legitimate power belonged to the people, whereas their neighbours went through numerous careful transitional stages, with continual reassuring references to God and their ancestors.

In France the republican state thus assumed from the outset a mission of emancipation, with the aim of introducing into every stratum of society the change of principles that had been achieved at the pinnacle of the state. Resistance, on the one hand, to these innovations from on high; and, on the other, enthusiastic adoption thereof: the whole tapestry of France's modern history has been woven from this duality. As heir of the Enlightenment and bearer of emancipation, the republican state was to a great extent suspicious of independent social expression. Control over education to the point of quasi-monopoly; struggle against regional cultures, languages and dialects, regarded as obscurantist; reduction in the influence of the religious Orders; preservation of the prerogatives of public authority; a fragile status, long maintained, for civil servants; control of the *départements* by powerful technical administrations dominated by the *'grands corps'*; the fact that the Rights of Man, the heart of the republican religion, failed until recently to provide for any appeal by citizens – all these features are symptoms of a centralized state, the agent of emancipation from above, somewhat authoritarian and in that respect, no doubt, not so different from its predecessors.

Centralist and authoritarian as it was, the republican state was nevertheless unable to establish itself permanently, in 1876, without restricting its field of competence – renouncing, in particular, any intervention in the economic and social domain. The Republic which in 1792 and 1848 had, by the very logic of its functioning – by the overthrow of the traditional authorities and by the opportunity given to the poor to voice their demands – shaken the social order, now agreed, through Gambetta, to define itself as conservative. What Stanley Hoffmann has called 'the republican compromise' signified a self-limitation of French democracy, whose political and cultural radicalism stopped short of social justice. This was the basis for an alliance between the business bourgeoisie and the provincial grandees who controlled political power. It was the origin of a paradoxical political system in which public life was politically revolutionary (struggle against traditionalist reaction, separation of Church and state) but socially conservative (the social achievements of the Third Republic by 1914 looked paltry compared with those of Lloyd George in Great Britain or Bismarck in Germany) and the electoral majority ('no enemies on the Left') had difficulty in recognizing itself in the governmental majority, which turned its back on the extreme Left and often admitted the Right into its ranks. This arrangement made it possible to mitigate what had been sudden and traumatic in the birth of democracy in France. Its effects were felt for a long time in the relations between state and society.

The 'stalemate society' appeared to be the counterpart of the republican synthesis: paralysis of capacity for reform owing to a political alliance in which the republican bourgeoisie was constantly in government while the socialist Left was neutralized, and no possibility of the emergence of a social-democratic movement. After the Commune, Gambetta chose to exclude the working-class movement from the political game, and that movement itself was caught in a trap. Obliged in every crisis (the *Boulangiste* movement, the Dreyfus affair) and even at every election, to support the Republic, even though the Republic was conservative, it was unable either to participate permanently in a majority government or to build an identity for itself through frank opposition to the Republican Party. The essential difference between France on the one hand and Britain or Germany on the other lies in the fact that because it was from the very outset (during the French Revolution) involved in the struggle for power, the French working-class movement has always been weak and divided. We see this in the history of the quarrels between tendencies among our Socialists – Guesdists against Jaurèsists, and so on – and also in the distance, more marked in France than in any other Western European country, between the trade-union movement and the political Left, which is always suspected by revolutionary trade unionists of wishing to secure a place in the republican political set-up, and so betray its principles.

Given these conditions, only marginal figures in the political system have attempted social breakthroughs – men like the progressive republican Léon Bourgeois or the former Socialist Alexandre Millerand – and they had tremendous difficulty in finding support. Ultimately it was often governments of the Right which carried out reforms – without, of course, the slightest participation by the social movement. The weakness of the labour movement has been cruelly exposed by its inability to construct a wide-ranging plan that could serve as a basis for a governmental alliance. In this connection the absence of detail in the programme of the People's Front, along with the earlier SFIO 'planning proposals' earlier failure to materialise, are revealing. Since there is no mature synthesis in society itself, the field is open for a variety of alliances formed between administration and the sectors under their supervision. This practice of specific alliances results, as some political sociologists (Pierre Grémion and Bruno Jobert) have pointed out, in the creation of a network of corporations, each with its own rules, self-esteem and privileges, and in a fragmentation of the state machine, infiltrated and 'turned over' like an octopus grabbed by its tentacles, by representatives of the very society which it is supposed to supervise.

At the end of the Third Republic, the republican state is a gigantic paradox. A secularization unparalleled in any other Western country made it the sole representative of civic values (which explains the disarray of the French when, in 1940, the state let them down). But this state, symbolically overloaded, fell into a passive torpor. It enjoyed a revolutionary glory, yet was not reforming. It pursued protectionist, even preservationist, social policies, effected through compromises, often static, that the state machine entered into with the grandees – territorial, as in the case of the engineers of the Highways Department; or sectoral, as in the case of social action. One could say, with Hoffmann, that there was 'adoption and protection of the corporate interests of the groups under administrative supervision [tutelle] by the administration exerting it', while, reciprocally, the representatives of these interests 'internalized the logic of the civil service'.[1] But this symbiosis, this adjustment through interpenetration, essentially had the effect of maintaining the established equilibria.

France is not unique in having such relations between state and corporations, but these characteristic features of its history have all too often been perceived only superficially, and this has put obstacles into the path of reform.

SEVEN

Modernizers of the Republic

In 1945 restoration of the state was not only General de Gaulle's obsession – it was shared by the mass of the French people, including those whom the republican system had marginalized. At that moment the word 'Republic' was common property, and no longer the label of a particular party. This unanimity at the Liberation had nothing to do with any nostalgia for the Third Republic. On the contrary, people vied with one another in denouncing the mediocre conservative compromises, the turgid electoral manoeuvres, the timid ambiguities in which the Radical-Socialists had indulged. Adherence to the Republican idea was linked with opposition to the prewar system. In contrast to traditional 'Republican politics' it signified a return to the 'mystique' of the Republic, as symbolized in its motto: Liberty, Equality, Fraternity. This renewal materialized in the economic and social reforms undertaken by the Republic. All those whom the conservative Republic had shouldered aside – Catholics, Socialists and Communists – participated in this second foundation. Let us note what was distinctive about the French model of democratic renewal in 1945 – *not*, as in Britain, the political emergence of the labour movement, but national unity, derived from the Resistance, around the restored state.

The republican mystique, the feeling of practical and moral responsibility borne by the state, particularly distinguished a generation of senior civil servants who, before the war, had vehemently criticized the incoherence and mediocrity of the political world, but now rejected the suspicions they had often heaped upon democracy in earlier days. The idea which inspired these modernizing technocrats – an idea derived from such precedents as the way the war economy functioned in 1914–18 – was to bring economic and social development into the sphere of state responsibility, transforming the state's role from conservative and protective to dynamic.

This change of direction by the state machine might momentarily have given grounds for believing in the possibility of a sort of social-democracy *à la française*. In the margin of a political process burdened with the task of liquidating France's colonial past, the public authorities drew the social partners into an anti-Malthusian compromise – development in exchange for social progress. Unfortunately, this consensus soon proved to be superficial. The ideology of modernization – not only material, but also in social and industrial relations – remained the property of an elite.[1] For lack of a sufficiently representative social organization, there was a failure to start a process of re-examining analyses, conduct, and the nature of demands.

Inside the administration itself, a gulf soon opened between 'conservative practicians' and 'interventionist modernizing technocrats' who were the less competent in that they did not enjoy support from the practicians.[2] Once the reconstruction period was over (when brutal necessity had made inevitable certain decisions such as those concerning infrastructures and basic industries in the Plan) the 'modernists' fell back upon missionary administrations concentrated upon specific objectives, or into parallel structures which, though not without capacities for innovation, marginalized them.

It became harder and harder to make uncontroversial choices. The big prestige operations, like Concorde or Fos, and some options which, a priori, could not be left to individual implementation (motorways, telephones) left public opinion bewildered. In fact, the credibility of the higher administration, which had reached its zenith after the Mendès-France period, began to crumble from the beginning of the Fifth Republic onwards. The term 'technocrat' acquired a pejorative meaning which reflected a vague sense of abuse of power and unjustified pretensions to ability to predict the future.

The failure of the modernizing administration to effect a thoroughgoing change in social behaviour had consequences even more serious than its difficulties with the administrators and their public. In this connection the decisive crisis occurred with the miners' strike of 1963 and the collapse of intentions to introduce an incomes policy (twenty-five years later, no one dares to utter those words). The system of social relations revealed its total abhorrence of the idea of a global compromise included in a set of objectives accepted by everyone. Corporatism, conflicting interests and balances of power, and the mobilization of public opinion, were to continue for a long time to provide the basis for the strategies of groups advancing their sectoral demands.

Actually, although the modernization party was strong enough within the administration to defend certain economic choices effectively (for example the major public investments, against Pinay's Malthusianism in 1958–9), it did not have enough outlets in politics and society to instigate a modernization of attitudes and social relations and, in particular, an awareness of the constraints imposed by the various forms of internationalization. The Mendès-France interlude had left the memory of a special moment when there had been a positive synergy between an active state restored to dignity, organized social forces called upon to enter into innovatory compromises, and a public opinion which had emerged from defensive pessimism and obsession with decline. It might have been thought that General de Gaulle's accession to power would make possible a repetition of the miracle, under much better conditions of stability, but disappointment was proportionate to expectation. On the contrary, the Fifth Republic saw the modernizers sink into increasing disarray.

The conditions under which de Gaulle returned to power were to handicap all his social plans, promoting in the Left camp an exasperation which made it overwhelmingly unreceptive to any innovatory approach. The fact that the General's political legitimacy was repeatedly confirmed by referendums did not alter the fact that he was cut off from a very large section of society's representatives. The modernizers were unable to find in the Gaullism of that time the roots, the mediations, which would have allowed their demands to become embodied in a political culture. Their initiatives were thus more exposed than ever before to the criticism (which exploded in May 1968) that they were ignorant of society, with all its diversity and richness. In the 1960s and 1970s it was against the apostles of rational management that social mobilization rose up, in forms that were more and more radical and less and less amenible to institution.

The crisis – that is to say, the sudden breaching, amidst the greatest disorder in the international monetary and commercial system, of a threshold in the process of globalization – struck France at the worst possible moment. We were in a state of utter euphoria, utter illusion. The inflationary growth of the Pompidou era was systematically exploited to prevent any questions being raised about social change, any idea of reform. Our society was 'running along its track, accumulating difficulties before it was obliged to change direction'.[3] A striking symptom of this French drama was the fact that twice (Chirac in 1974, Mauroy in 1981) the rulers had recourse to the old quantity-theory drug, pump-priming, so as not to be obliged to think about what lay beneath the country's problems.

And what lay beneath those difficulties was – and still is – the relatively superficial character of modernization as carried out in France, which gives more priority to technical feats than to useful production and the development of individual capacities, or at least shows itself too quickly satisfied with feats, however necessary these may be. There is also the split between the elites who are conscious – or claim to be conscious – of the scale of the issues at stake and the politicians, who are always accused of routinism, as if our political or industrial system were incapable of conceiving proper, dialectical apprenticeship processes, in which top and bottom mutually instruct each other, so as to produce a more flexible and more precise competence. The welfare state suffers more than any other sector of activity from this compartmentalizing of knowledge, since its objective should be the emancipation of the weak and dependent. The difficulty of breaking through bureaucratic isolationism and frontiers between specializations, and the scant readiness for debate, render permanent – especially in the social domain – the corporatisms within society and the fragmentation of the state.

Contrary to what happens in other countries, the French social system functions more by accumulating *ad hoc* measures than by developing public services, reflecting a lack of collective capacity to tackle problems. This is seen also in the largely passive treatment of unemployment. As for health insurance, this, instead of concerning itself with the effectiveness of care, operates as a redistribution of contributions. There are contributors and claimants, but not much of a strategy for improving health, yet there is no lack of competence in this sphere. The absence of a collective will results in a complete desocializing of social problems, which are viewed exclusively in terms of allocations which have to be shared out among individuals. Hence the split, which is especially marked in the French attitude, between the economic and the social, between the individual producer and the individual consumer.

For lack of constructive vision, the social aspect is experienced as a series of lacks, of things that are wrong, of risks to be compensated for, instead of being thought of as a space in which to promote human qualities and liberate productive capacities. It was this passive conception of the social aspect that caused the comparative failure of the modernization undertaken by the renewed republican state of the postwar period. Our society swings between sporadic mobilization against the authorities or the employers and silent, depressed suffering when, as now, it seems that revolt would be futile, but there is no longer any feeling that society is the active partner of the various authorities.

EIGHT

Non-transferable Models

Pᴇᴏᴘʟᴇ are very ready to offer the French two examples for a rethinking of the way in which the state and society should be linked: the social-democratic example and that of the liberal state (meaning mainly the USA).

In comparison with the logic of France's institutions, the historical characteristics which have marked the social democracies count for a great deal. The Scandinavian countries did not experience to the same extent the destabilization of the social authorities that was caused elsewhere by the conditions in which democracy was established. The German countries have repressed like a nightmare the memory of that destabilization (the Weimar Republic, Austria between the world wars, Nazism), and it is the legitimacy that has been maintained or recovered by major social forces (trade unions, vast and non-specialized associations, churches) that are independent of the state, but share the public arena with it, which has made possible in German-speaking Europe a certain form of social dialogue.

The gap is so wide between French realities and – not the values, but the historical facts which underlie the social democracies, that invoking *that* model amounts to little more than gloomy rhetoric:

ah, if only France were not what she is, if her history had been different, if Francis I had opted for the Reformation. . . . The problem clearly does not lie there. It is useless to dream of changing one's skin: useless, for example, to suppose that the French state could be anywhere but at the centre of our public domain. If one wants to change its role, that can be done only by acknowledging, not by denying, its importance.

This criticism applies *a fortiori* to the liberals' proposals, which share with the social-democratic proposals the requirement that the state should withdraw to give way, in their case, not to an internal compromise in a self-organized society but rather to free individual decisions.

Actually, the idea of a perfectly neutral state cannot hold water. It looks realistic only in so far as society retains, in practice, beneath nominal pluralism, an adherence to certain common values, especially religious ones, to which, as in the United States, the state does not fail to pay tribute. It is due to the strength of the religious substratum that in the USA it is possible to seem unaware that all the modern democracies are based on the operation of certain common values, and not merely on the recognition of individual rights. The presence of the word 'fraternity' in our republican motto means that every citizen has a duty to help others equally to be citizens and, to that end, to enjoy instruction, information, security, and all the other basic rights. The liberals are correct when they say that the representative state cannot answer for individual morality, but they are wrong when they forget that democracy necessarily aims at a form of political commonweal, a domain of strictly political morality – the duty of every citizen, as also of the citizens as a body, to see to it that others can develop as individuals. The duty of practical solidarity is consubstantial with democracy. Even though it had a different orientation, was not Reaganism an example of moral interventionism by the highest expression of the state?

We shall therefore get nowhere if we try to regard the specific character of France, where the role of the state is concerned, as a pernicious aberration. Our republican state seems to be more loaded with values than others. If the collective memory assigns a special place to those – de Gaulle, Mendès-France – who have brought a moral content into political activity, this is because the unavoidable idea of the public good, represented elsewhere by other institutions (churches, a monarchy, foundations, universities, a supreme court) is for us crystallized mainly around executive power. This situation creates a problem. There is some truth in the complaint of those for whom the French-type state, by monopolizing concern for the general interest, infantilizes society and thrusts the ordinary citizen back into private life. However, the solution lies neither in the concept of a state free from any moral values nor in transferring concern for justice and solidarity to non-state institutions. The heart of the problem lies in the way the state's centrality is linked with other initiatives. The classical republican state was not a solitary monster. It sometimes knew how to mobilize its servants (the 'black hussars'), and it also knew how to co-operate with the grandees. What we must do, then, is to find new forms for a genuine synergy between society and the state.

NINE

State and Society: Towards a New Synergy

I F WE emphasize, as we have just done, the historical roots of the French model, this does not mean we deny that it is in crisis: on the contrary, it means we are trying to understand the depth of this crisis. After the Pompidou and Giscard periods, the Left's accession to power may be seen as a sort of return to the source, a republican revival, an attempt to restore and extend the state as educator, the state which is ahead of society and for which the organized forces of the 'people of the Left' should act as outlets. The stagnation we are now in results directly from the failure of that attempt.

The setbacks suffered by the Left are due, over and above material restrictions, to the delegitimation that the state has encountered. Nothing more will be said here about economic constraint, but it should be noted that the most virulent protest against austerity has arisen in connection with the restriction on foreign travel, a sign of the vulnerability of the national stronghold. Another, more serious diminution of the state, in the cultural sphere, is the Left's action in conceding the fifth television channel to Silvio Berlusconi, which struck a decisive blow at public-service television, an essential symbol of the state as educator. Even in the

57

juridical sphere the French state has had to yield parts of its sovereignty to European regulation and the Luxembourg Court of Justice. Just think – one can no longer nationalize or privatize in peace within the Hexagon!

No less striking has been the internal delegitimation of the state. The private schools affair marked the apogee of this process. The implicit argument which brought victory to the cause of 'free' education may be put like this: since democracy has been established irreversibly in France, and the theologico-political conflict begun in 1789 is over and done with, the state's mission of political education is now pointless. French society has at last reached maturity, and those in the FEN [the state-school teachers' union] who assert an exclusive claim to the Republic are at least somewhat behind the times. Given that republican values are shared by parish priests as well as village schoolteachers, the latter have no right to demand the monopoly of education which the Left's plans seemed to be preparing for them. Supporters of secular education must accept the fact that their opponents are also within the Republic, and that in this particular case the Debré Act, by imposing respect for freedom of conscience on officially recognized establishments, implemented a certain unification of the French cultural system. In short, it is because – largely as a result of Gaullism – a degree of consensus on political values has been attained that the state's claim to educate society can now be challenged. Does reality conform to this argument, throughout the sphere of private education? That is another matter. But this argument was what constantly underlay the embittered rhetoric of the defenders of the private sector and, along with parents' wish to have an alternative in the event of disappointment with state schools, it hit home.

On another plane, the Constitutional Council wins approval whenever it sets limits to the actions of the legislature, and public opinion readily goes along with the tendency, through the creation of independent bodies of the Higher Authority type (or the CNCL [*Commission Nationale de la Communication et des Libertés* – a governmental commission set up to regulate the media], if that had not failed in its task), to guarantee pluralism and curtail the government's powers. Now that the French no longer doubt that their democracy is securely anchored, they are less willing to tolerate state militancy and the assumption of public authority for their own ends by those politicians who happen to be in power. Political activism used to aim at increasing state power; today, it is the other way round. The idea of a state under supervision, a somewhat diminished state, goes along with the idea that the ordinary citizen feels and expresses democratic values better than the professionals do. Some paradoxes follow from this. At the end of 1986 it was by appealing to the most classical democratic values that students and secondary-school pupils succeeded in bullying representative democracy. By attacking the Chirac government and its majority, they separated the state from the political values it had hitherto monopolized. The same way of assuming that democratic values are widespread in society is characteristic of the activity of movements like *SOS Racisme* or Amnesty International. The *Ligue des Droits de l'Homme*, an organization born in a different epoch, always refers, when it takes a stand on some matter, to the democratic ideal which must be established and to the political struggles necessary to combat latent obscurantism. Movements of more recent origin appeal to commonly held values: the general condemnation of torture and deprivation of political freedom, and the values of interracial tolerance that prevail in the culture of our teenagers.

The difficulty of restoring the French state effectively is apparent. The Left's messianic and reformist attempts have come up against the same resistance as the intentions of the Right. The state finds itself subject not only to international constraints but also to checks by public opinion – a new, vague and unstable, force in politics which the media crystallize or caricature much more than they shape, and whose verdicts are often final. While, however, the state's freedom of movement is restricted, in the political domain, as in the economic, the crisis merely intensifies the demands from various groups for protection, and the requirements of solidarity. Diminished scope for controlling the economy, rejection by public opinion of a state that sees itself as being above or ahead of society, the continued, even perhaps increasing, strength of the requirement of solidarity – we can see, when we list these constraints, that the entire apparatus for action must be reviewed. What we can say is that the state, having worked for political emancipation under the Third Republic and Gaullism, now has to play the social card, in a way that allows for the crisis of the welfare state. In 1981, as under Pompidou, it was believed that all that was necessary was to assert political control over the economy and its growth, and the protection or reform of society would follow. Today the order of these factors is reversed. Economics turns out to be secondary to social organization – a way of mobilizing human resources, not merely a distribution system. The art of politics has to concern itself with concentrating energy in the interests of preserving shared values and the nation's chances of maintaining its historical role.

Since our society has taken the measure of the monstrous aberrations of totalitarianism and the lack of realism in traditionalisms and all closed conceptions of society, it knows the worth of the values that inspire it. It is not interested in a state which tries to excite it by promising victory over obscurantism, or perfect justice. The unifying social movements, cutting across categories, which, combined with political power, made possible in the social-democratic countries both the institutionalizing of conflicts and the compromises to anticipate them, had their source in a utopian vision of a different society. France, where the labour movement has never possessed much capacity for institutionalizing conflicts, lends itself less than ever to movements of that sort. The innovative initiatives of today are based not upon the idea of a different society but on fundamental shared values, whether it is a matter of reminding the state of their existence (the activities of *SOS Racisme*, the movement in defence of minorities) or contributing to their implementation (solidarity initiatives). The problem consists not of mass conflicts (conflicts over values or social conflicts) but of apathy, incapacity, exclusion. The objective, therefore, is not so much to conclude armistices as to activate, economically and socially, those sectors which are neglected by society, those who are deprived of participation.

The new social expressions outline a new place for the state. These movements cannot be 'taken over' politically, nor do they herald a social alternative which some power ought to establish. They emanate from a society which is grown up and accepts itself as it is, while being aware of the imperfect and perfectible nature of any realization of its values. On an equal footing with the state, they should be able to watch over the latter and help it to accomplish its task. The classical social movements were movements of 'placard-carriers', to quote Jacques Donzelot. They raised social questions to the level of politics and, by their pressure, effected a kind of trickle into the sphere of state power. Today's movements already proceed in the opposite direction, bearing witness to society's takeover of political values, the diffusion of the political in the social. They aim to secure new forms of co-operation, obliging the state to share the political arena. They want to contribute solutions, and they take a direct share in solving the problems that gave rise to their own existence.

In order to adapt itself to this new deal – or at least to as much of it as is apparent among the signs of disappointment (the 'negative dialectic' of state and society) or even despair (the chauvinist backlash, a nationalism which in fact rejects national values) – the state must present itself, at the symbolic as at the political level, as a declericalized state which represents shared values without monopolizing them, agrees to be supervised and to co-operate, and illustrates democracy all the better for submitting to it.

In practice, renunciation of the monopoly of values entails transition from a heavily burdened protector-state, whose paternalism incites everyone to demand as many rights and as few responsibilities as possible (this being the only way of asserting oneself in a system which leaves the subject with no power of initiative), to the animator-state outlined by Donzelot, which would organize, in relation to the problems to be solved (unemployment, integration of young and old into society, deliquency), co-operation and confrontation between public services, elected administration, and associations. The 'inter-partnership' would break down the little socio-administrative islands which characterize the French system, cut the closed circuit between an administration and the representatives (manipulated or manipulating) of its territory, and compel all to emerge from their reserves, since the task would be, under the supervision of the elected administration, to deal with a problem, rather than manage a situation. The initiatives for the integration of young people created by Bertrand Schwartz and the Bonnemaison Commission on Deliquency have shown the possible nature of the procedures which, by changing administrative behaviour, could open the way to new relations between state and society.

In the present atmosphere of disappointment and anti-state demagogy we may fear the pauperization, degradation or even collapse of a state whose role has not been reviewed. Because it is sinking under a mass of duties with which it can no longer cope, the French state lacks the necessary freedom of manoeuvre.[1] Consequently, the choice is clear: either it withdraws and renounces the assumption of solidarity, thereby incurring the risk of compromising its legitimacy, or it finds partners in society to help it change social attitudes of suffering and moaning into social activity. In the second case, the state must re-examine and revitalize its principal functions:

• The *forecasting* function. A plain proof of the state's decline since the Pompidou era is that its intellectual mechanisms – and, first and foremost, its planning apparatus – have disintegrated. Now the state's primary function is to enable a nation to confront its historical situation. To do so it must unceasingly check on and deepen the country's awareness of this situation, in relation both to itself and to the outside world. One of the most negative effects of the liberal wave may well be a renunciation of collective responsibility for the strategic task, the task of anticipation which, for the people, is the condition of success, if it is true, as Simone Weil wrote, that 'if we do not know what is possible and what is impossible, life is merely a shameful delirium.'

• The *deliberation* function. The capacity for deliberation is stifled both by our polemical traditions and by a certain intellectual conformism of the press and the cultural elites. Bringing up a given problem already means taking one side or the other. Here in France we do not accept the other side's questions. Anyone who

says that immigration or public pornography constitutes a problem is liable to be taken for a filthy racist or an intolerant Pharisee.
Since problems cannot be solved by keeping quiet about them,
they do in fact get dealt with, but discreetly and even clandestinely,
until demagogic pressures or political manoeuvres bring them to
the forefront in an artificial or dangerous fashion. The parliamentary framework, the natural setting for democratic deliberation,
has lost almost all its relevance. It might recover that relevance
through a policy of great debates using the work of the intellectual
nuclei of the administration (such as the Foreign Ministry's Centre
for Analysis and Forecasting) and that of the various organizations,
public or even private, which are concerned with observation and
prediction. Political life would thus renew its ties with intellectual
life and the social debate. How many ill-prepared reforms have
failed because the parliamentarians had wrongly calculated the
state of public opinion . . .! Moreover, a debate within the institutions is not enough – citizens must also be involved.

Paradoxically, it is the decline in political passions that necessitates the promotion of wider deliberation processes. The present
electoral system, two-coloured if not two-party, reflects only very
crudely the variety and shades of opinion among our citizens. The
rulers thus need parallel processes of inquiry and confrontation
which will enable them to measure actual opinions, and also to
change these opinions. They are aware of this, as we see from the
commissions of wise men on immigration, for example, or the
States General of social security. But these are as yet only rustlings,
and perhaps mere excuses. Besides, democracy would gain nothing if a commission were to claim to settle that question once and
for all. Society's major problems evolve more often than they get
settled. Deliberation learns to live with them, free from any
neurotic attitude, and this is already a way of dealing with them.
Democracy is not the art of ridding ourselves of problems, but
rather a permanent process of deliberation, with decisions being
made along the way.

• The *evaluation* function. In France the state is both judge and
party to disputes.[2] The administration evaluates itself, sovereignly

(which means that it does *not* evaluate itself), while setting itself up as judge of the administered. Being both too indirect and too all-embracing, political supervision cannot really be effective. It is important to create a system which appreciates administrative performance in relation to objectives (whose definition is the prerogative of the political authorities) and takes account of customers' complaints. There are examples: Sweden's 'state control', Japan's Management and Co-ordination Agency, or even, in France, the Laurent Schwartz Commission for evaluating the universities. Subjecting the organs of the state to evaluation means forcing it not only to break with routine but also to rationalize its activity, and making it capable of co-operating better in this activity with outside forces, without this necessarily resulting either in the infiltration of the administration by private interests or in the colonization of society by administrative ambitions.

The three functions outlined above tend, in the same way, to prompt administrative activity to stand back a little from itself, to distinguish between the majesty of public power and the tentative modesty of its actions, and both to decide on its aims, under supervision by public opinion and the electorate, and then to check publicly on the extent to which these aims have been achieved. By agreeing to function in this way, the state would assert itself as the representative and guarantor or shared values while also acknowledging its equality with the other components of society when it comes to putting these values into practice. Having stepped down from its pedestal and undertaken to engage in real co-operation with the interests and energies which make up society, such a state would cease to be the scapegoat of our disappointments and powerlessness.

A culture of solidarity

The idea that the state should be, *de jure* or *de facto*, ahead of society is a collective belief that has underlain French political life for two centuries. It has been incarnated in two figures: the state as educator

64

(whose job the French seem now to think is a different one) and the state as protector (which no longer has the means to do its job). The state as protector has long known how to reconcile innovations that were the work of minorities with safeguarding traditional values and ways of life.

In French tradition, solidarity has been ensured by one's membership of a group of people like oneself who appeal to a higher level (in the last analysis, the state) for protection. The locus of membership was dissociated from the locus of guarantee. The affective and effective dimensions of solidarity were separated. From the moment, however, when the guaranteeing authority shows itself to be powerless, or at least inadequate, the group, now exposed to attack from outside, goes into crisis. It either collapses or becomes rigid, taking the ultimate and dramatic form of an exclusive brotherhood, an impervious corporatism. Or else – a third possibility – it opens itself up, tries to find its place in society, and negotiates conditions that will allow it to exist and its members to be protected. In that third case the group itself assumes responsibility, and guarantee is integral to membership; whereas before, the burden had been shifted elsewhere. In other words, solidarity, instead of being thought of in terms of individual rights, is perceived rather as a collective obligation. The obligation, consubstantial with democracy, to ensure for everyone whatever is needed for the exercise of citizenship – that is, for living a full life – cannot be guaranteed by the state or, indeed, by anyone at all, because its fulfilment depends on many different contingencies, both material and moral. Yet it is up to everyone (collectively and individually) to try to perform this task. Because the task is infinite and success in it is precarious, the obligation of solidarity cannot be placed wholly on the shoulders of the state: it concerns all who belong to 'the city'. Its achievement cannot be ensured once and for all, because it calls for an infinite series of initiatives which confer a style on social life, that of fellow-citizenship taken seriously. The 'good' society is not one in which everybody has everything he or she needs; such an ideal would be more appropriate to a well-run ranch than to a society of human beings. The good society is one in which need is recognized and the fact that other people are frustrated creates an obligation which is both experienced and organized.

Closed memberships and exclusive brotherhoods go with the idea of a provider-state, able to supply whatever is needed – a state which is thought of as all-powerful, a state whose actions, by virtue of the 'prerogatives of public authority' (as administrative law has it), possess greater value and legitimacy than those of any other element in society. If, contrariwise, the obligation of solidarity concerns all authorities, both political and social, what is needed is a state that is in synergy with society. Even if the state lacks the means to realize all the ideas of democracy, it must not, despite what the liberals say, take no interest in them. It must, at the very least, incarnate them, remind people of them, indicate them as reference points for social effort. Instead of substituting itself for society in its moral obligations, the solidarity state makes these obligations more immediately present. When it describes society's situation, forecasts how it will evolve, and stimulates and co-ordinates initiatives to meet future needs, it intervenes so as to activate the sense of responsibility which it symbolizes.

A society in which the state is no mere excuse but is attentive to frustrated needs is also more agile economically, better able to effect the redeployments called for by the crisis. This is, above all, a question of developing the economy in the direction of personal services. However, if one is to be able to invent the economic mechanisms which will make it possible to respond to the needs of culture and needs which are due to more widespread loneliness or an ageing population, these needs must previously have been given adequate attention; they must have been recognized in both senses of the word – that is to say, explored and also judged to be important, accorded legitimacy. It can be said that the progress of social consciousness and the perception of latent needs form the indispensable substratum for the success of economic reorientations.

This conditioning of the economic by the social is doubtless to be found even in the supply of services. Certain examples (crèches in which parents help with the work, or care for old people in their own homes) give us reason to think that the development of some services is economically possible only if an element of voluntary work comes into play, influencing the creation of certain jobs in so far as it reduces the cost, public or private, of the services rendered. The line between waged work and voluntary work could also be crossed by combining, in accordance with the model offered by the TUC [*travaux d'utilité collectif* – a form of community service], the right to receive certain allowances (early-retirement pension, unemployment pay) with the obligation, in exchange, to give up some of one's time to the performance of services which it is hard to finance otherwise, such as prison-visiting, helping some children with their schoolwork, drawing old people into social life, and so on. Could not the social guarantee a person enjoys be linked with a personal involvement in solidarity? Such proposals doubtless call for mediation by specialized associations capable of generating the necessary motivation.

One aspect of the 'service orientation' of the economy is the development of personal services which do not always call for a high level of skill. What kind of supply can correspond to this kind of demand? Either a workforce that is poorly paid and without much protection, on the Reaganite model, or (why not, if one thinks of the 'opportunities' created by immigration?) a workforce with a status akin to that of slaves. Or there could be systems which link voluntary work with waged work, either subsidized or not, in a solidaristic framework. In any case if there is no clear choice of some coherent form of halfway house between available energies and recognized needs, unemployment can only increase and needs can only be left unsatisfied.

The reigning tendency today is to conceive of no activity that is not carried out with a view to remuneration. Even the work of housewives and parents lacks genuine recognition by society. We have a narrow conception of human activity. The question is whether it is possible to bring within the framework of that single status all the activities that correspond to human needs. Without going so far as to concern ourselves with demands so personal as those for love or friendship, it is clear that, in the future, demand will be to an ever greater extent non-material, relational and even affective. The form and status of every activity will have to be adapted to this new deal, or we shall see frustration and even misery increase along with leisure. Perhaps the very development of the market presumes a society more open to cultural and moral needs – that is to say, the development of activities which, so to speak, give form and legitimacy to these 'moral' needs which will occupy an increasingly important place, and make them economically manageable. The social-democratic countries' resistance to unemployment is due in part to the vitality of their social fabric, which is able to recognize and deal with needs that are disregarded elsewhere.

The individualistic nature of modern societies is crystallized in a system of laws (wages, pensions, insurance) which are linked, whether directly or not, with work. This system will not be challenged: we shall not go back to a communal culture. But since the obligation of solidarity – which is, moreover, indissociable from the principle of individualism (meaning that everyone must be a fully fledged individual) – cannot be wholly fulfilled through any mere mechanical redistribution, the problem becomes one of linking the system of individual rights with the necessary involvement of people and groups in implementing this obligation. The idea of a social duty that is incumbent not only on 'society' but also on every single person inevitably compels acceptance when the development of individuals is acknowledged to be the common aim. The movement which leads to a 'resituating' of the state, putting it not so much above society as *with* society, must be included within the framework of this deepening of the moral and solidarist aspect of the democratic idea.

TEN

The Challenge of Economic Performance

'COMPETITIVENESS: Say, with a gloomy air, that it is insufficient.' That is what one might find, in the style of Flaubert, in a modern *Dictionary of Received Ideas*. The competitiveness of French – and, indeed, of European – business[1] is not a matter of choice. It is a requirement that must be met if we are to combine, in a positive way, an opening on to the outside world with progress in society.

In brief, competitiveness means the group of factors which enable a company or a country to struggle on equal terms with its competitors and, if possible, to overcome them. Victory or defeat – to stay with this appropriately warlike tone – is not measured merely in economic terms. Everyone has been aware, since the beginning of the 1970s, that the constraints of competition cause havoc in the social fabric. Consequently, the choice before us is clear. Either the achievement of a satisfactory level of competitiveness is seen as an end in itself, with the reconstitution of social structures as a sort of spontaneous by-product, or the two go together, the one feeding on the other. This is the big challenge for anyone claiming to respond to the needs and expectations of the French people. Is this a Sisyphean illusion? Not necessarily. The upheavals that affect economic competitiveness contain unprecedented opportunities for the world of labour to exert influence, through business, on the way the present is managed and on the choices to be made in the future. The more workers become actors on the economic stage, the more profit and prerogatives they will derive from it and the more, at the same time, they will contribute towards improving it. The coin has, of course, another side. Fresh dangers arise. Participation by workers must deprive them neither of their individual freedom nor of their collective capacity to negotiate effective compensation for flexibility.

The essential question, therefore, is to clarify the new conditions for competitiveness. The whole of the Western world is faced with the same changes and trying to solve the same problems, but there are many differences in situations and conditions. Understanding our specific handicaps and taking steps to overcome them acquires significance in a context that we shall try to outline.

What performance depends on

All long-term studies show that competitiveness in world markets goes with a more and more highly qualified specialization, in an increasingly complex setting of products, services and technologies. The most profitable market positions are only temporary and result from a particular combination of resources and know-how that an enterprise has managed to mobilise. This enterprise has to be permanently capable of creating new combinations that will be rich and dynamic enough to take advantage of opportunities as they arise; otherwise, yesterday's success quickly brings about today's defeat. Even the most powerful lords of world industry are subject to this rule.

The costs of research, development and transition to industrial production are rising sharply. Whatever the position in question, the 'entrance ticket' costs millions of dollars.

The life cycle of products gets shorter. The share of investment devoted to grey matter increases faster than the minimal useful amount of total investment. Consequently, access to information, or possession of it, acquires strategic importance and necessitates a strong emphasis on qualifications. The place and role of labour in the economy of production and services change profoundly. The importance of services in economic activity as a whole increases – which does not mean that society can get by without basing its development on scientific and industrial dynamism. On the contrary, progress in competitiveness and employment requires solid productive foundations. Even though the fast-food economy has been responsible for creating many jobs in the United States in recent years, a large proportion of the new services are directly connected with industry. Moreover, in the most advanced sectors, the old frontiers between industry and services no longer signify.

What will be the place of France, and of Europe, in future economic production? What prospect of strategic acceleration in mergers and international alliances does it hold out for our enterprises? How will labour and employment evolve, threatened as they are by a split between the strong and the weak, those who gain from competitiveness and the victims of precariousness? What economic policy is appropriate to the choices that will have to be made? How will its objectives, its instruments and its means of operation be defined?

These questions are closely interconnected. Macroeconomic management is the prerogative of the political decision-makers, and what they do is not without effect, but on the national scale they enjoy only limited room for manoeuvre. As for France's enterprises, given our history and our industrial culture, we may fear that only the harshness of constraints of every kind will force them, in the main, to make a real entry into the game of worldwide trade. For these two reasons – and in order to avoid corruption of the social process through modernization – it seems to us that we need the all-European framework. The great internal market, the coming of which worries so many French business leaders, also has the merit of channelling the harshness of the economic environment.

Business in a changing landscape

The social body of a business may be compared to a living body. It is born and it dies, it grows or it suffers, it reaches maturity or it withers away. Its productive or commercial dynamism is inconceivable apart from the personal experiences and social debates that affect it. That inner well-spring of performance, the conscious adherence of the individuals and groups concerned to the company's objectives, presupposes a form of shared identity that nonetheless allows for differences and conflicts. The business has its roots, moreover, in territories whose resources help to give it shape. Complex products of a history, these realities, whether convergent or contentious, are lasting, and evolve at their own pace. But their environment is also evolving ceaselessly. The permanent confrontation between price and quality goes on at increasing speed, and operates on a global scale.

In the era of rapid transport, instant dissemination of information, weakening of barriers, the world of production is dominated by the fluidity of trade. The growing share of technology in added value and the explosion in research and development costs require that expenditure be recovered in at least two of the three great markets: North America, Europe and the Far East. The periodicity of economic cycles quickens and, for some goods, becomes irregular, giving rise to crises. The more fluidity intensifies, the more sudden are the variations.

It seems that the monetary factor is not enough to embody a nation's competitiveness; let us say that it symbolizes rather than defines it. At a deeper level, this competitiveness is related to a new definition of productivity, based largely on the skill, creativity and power of initiative and co-operation possessed by economic actors. Under present-day conditions, that definition could be broken down like this: trustworthiness, capacity for communication, structural fluidity of business, flexibility in their willingness to develop.

The trustworthiness of a company's products in terms of price, quality, delivery dates and services reassures its customers in a world dominated by uncertainty. It is demonstrated also through the security of industrial processes, technologies and sophisticated products. Reflected by public opinion and the media, it is decisive for the 'brand image' of the company, and even of the nation. One need only observe the prestige of the label 'Made in Germany', even in areas where, objectively, the quality of French goods is comparable.

Capacity for communication, internal or external, is dominated by the increasing role played by information and knowledge as productive, commercial and strategic resources. It proceeds principally from the will to make available and to exchange all useful information, which presupposes profound changes in nodes of relation and organization, and also effective use of information technology, which is advancing rapidly.

Structural fluidity depends on the willingness to regroup, to form alliances, to separate or relocate activities which change business frontiers and identities. Keeping to the biological comparison used above, we could say that it is a matter of surgery. It does not square with the classical patrimonial tradition, still less with the archaic forms of taxation and accounting which survive here and there. It implies the possession of financial capacities adequate for making such investments for external growth as may prove necessary. This financial component of industrial strategies is vital. It should not be confused with the fever of purely financial operations which has raged over these last few years in the industrialized countries, with consequences of which we are only too aware. Geographical fluidity can mean a number of different things. Knowing how to invest in a certain country or region is essential to getting into a better position even to approach a market. This also needs to be done in such a way as to benefit from more advantageous production costs or monetary conditions when competition from countries where such costs and conditions prevail proves threatening, though it must not become systematic and does not provide a long-term guarantee. At the present time this is one line of force in the strategy of the big Japanese groups which, fleeing from the overvalued yen and the increasing wage costs of their mother country, are transferring some of their production capacities to Korea, Taiwan, Singapore and Hong Kong, or even to the border between the USA and Mexico. Sony will soon be manufacturing more than a quarter of its products outside Japan. These are examples to be thought about, but not to be followed indiscriminately.

Internal flexibility takes many forms. As capacity to adapt to market changes it can help to safeguard or create many jobs. It concerns employment first and foremost, through adjustment of working hours and differential forms of employment, as well as length of time and flexibility in using equipment. It is shown in the way work is organized, and in modes of participation. However, the experience of recent years shows that this concept is difficult to handle. For some, flexibility means merely the opportunity to reduce the numbers employed, with no or little cost – in plain words, to 'slim'. For others, flexibility implies an arithmetical sharing of work which, when applied without reference to the economic conditions of the given activity, obviously does not produce the expected effects. Something else is possible. We shall return to this subject in the chapter on employment.

Strategic recentring and the archipelago

This set of conditions and factors already entails a remodelling of the structure of business, which is readily perceivable in the strategy of the big groups. Faced with the formidable dimensions of the investments and markets they need for their development, the largest firms refocus on the trades which offer them a leading position, with the opportunity to swing from one sector to another. To quote only one famous example: less than twenty years ago France's Number One in the agro-food business, BSN [Boussois-Souchon-Neuvesel], produced nothing but glass. Through taking an interest in the products that were put into its big bottles and little pots, BSN, which some time before had given up the manufacture of plate glass, became the king of yoghurt, mineral water and biscuits, and now appears under a different heading in the *Institut National de Statistiques et d'Etudes Economiques* (INSEE) classification. The same objective may also be realized by intensified and renewed specialization in the same sector.

The big groups also select the strategic functions of research, production and sale, form subsidiaries, engage in sub-contracting, and make external purchases or borrowings where complementary materials are concerned, sometimes including their own accounting and administrative services. Their more or less permanent remodelling usually entails reduction in numbers employed. The growing complexity of products and the size of the amounts at stake also result in an increasing interdependence between enterprises, which multiply their forms of alliance: joint ventures, all kinds of participation, subsidiaries and co-operation, covering the whole spectrum of activity from research to marketing. Alongside the classical form of subcontracting, one is struck by the rapid emergence of new small and medium-sized enterprises in the technological field, more or less dependent on the markets of the big groups. And, contrary to so-called liberal talk, a mobilization of public money is often crucial for the attainment of a satisfactory level of competitiveness, especially in activities connected with research or sales to government bodies.

The general features of these reconfigurations are to be found in every country. Every government influences the modalities and alliances that bear on the competitiveness of its country's industry. Not one of them stays out of this game. In France, industrial policy is practised openly and given its own name. In Japan, everyone knows that industry and finance, on the one hand, and the quasi-mythical MITI, on the other, have reached an almost perfect state of osmosis. In other countries the actual term 'industrial policy' does not exist, but it is practised without being talked about, and to no less an extent. And under a variety of forms American industry is sustained, guided and structured by federal funds and programmes.

How is one to obtain an overall view of these processes? How are good strategic choices to be made? For France, as for the other countries of the Community, this question is posed on the pan-European scale. Building the great internal market brings up the problem of Europe's specialization in the world economy and, consequently, that of how production is to be distributed within Europe. For those French enterprises – still numerous – which have not acquired the habit of conceiving their strategies in terms that reach beyond the 'Hexagon', it is going to be a hard struggle.

Human resources and the world of labour

Fundamentally, what is changing in the world of production is labour's relation to the production process. This applies to the manual labour reduced or externalized by automation, but it is also true of all the interdependent activities, ranging from conception to manufacture to sale, under the conditions of competition just described. The 'intelligence revolution' is bringing upheaval into the social no less than the economic situation. The conditions for mobilizing human activity are altered.

Without competitiveness, nothing can be done, but the new deal implicit in it means that previously existing social structures are dislocated. Entire sections of employment collapse. The proportion of people written off increases in direct ratio to the increase in unemployment. Other social cleavages and *rapprochements* begin to appear. Mobility and training for new trades are hindered by underemployment. An investigation carried out among 207 enterprises employing 1.6 million people in all showed that 59 per cent of the workers had been in the same job for more than ten years in 1985, compared with 47 per cent in 1979. The omnipresent threat of unemployment exerts a powerful social constraint, causing those who do have a job to hang on to it at all costs. Loyalty to a particular company is submitted to, not chosen. Participation becomes a new form of alienation. What advantages can the world of labour discover, then, in the new conditions of performance?

From inside the business, the reply is less necessarily negative. True, a great deal needs to be done, but one may be reassured to observe that in the economy of performance, quality of labour is beginning to be more important than quantity. This quasi-revolution contains within itself the beginnings of a change in social relations, in the meaning and object of conflicts and in the logic of compromise, which points towards emancipation, but it is still necessary for this change to be willed and organized. Based on the priority of quality, conscious support for whatever constitutes the object of co-operation between individuals and teams in the same company can favour the development of maturity and independence in the collective worker no less than the individuality and improvement of the individual person. The company's competitiveness needs this. Workers can find in it fertile soil for new forms of solidarity. It does not do away with the conflict between capital and labour but shifts it, in the long term, towards the strategic issue of capacity to direct the economy.

ELEVEN

The Evolving Enterprise

Loyalty and the individual

THE social animal enjoys a sort of positive schizophrenia. He has constant loyalty to a group, to society, and no less constantly marks himself off from them. The assertion of individuality is a primordial characteristic of European culture. Every individual is unique, but the history of every individual is rooted in a network of multiple memberships. The singularity of the individual is nourished by group cultures, and vice versa.

These mechanisms apply also in the enterprise, which is the locus of an essential membership. Pride in work and the product, the will to succeed, reaction to threats of competition, can all converge in a form of loyalty. 'Workplace patriotism' exists. A variety of realities and values mingle in this attachment. Competitive aggressivity and association in labour are both there, and not necessarily in opposition. The valorization of the individual through responsibility or through wages can be associated with agreement just as well as with competition between fellow-workers. The difficulty lies in establishing, or bringing to birth, a balance between these forces in such a way as to create good conditions for performance while at the same time guaranteeing a space, both individual and collective, for the workers. Although it is universally necessary to the world economy, the nature of this balance differs from one culture to another. There is much to be learnt on this score from the United States and Japan, provided one bears in mind that their business cultures, which themselves differ markedly, cannot constitute role models. Any attempt to transpose one or the other would mean certain defeat. It is the European productive model that has to be reinvented. Bringing out its lines of force is a political task that transcends the framework of the individual enterprise.

Training

Trades are changing. Appropriate skill has become a scarce resource. An enterprise cannot solve this problem on its own, because it is necessary to rethink and reformulate the education system.

Nevertheless, businesses have to foresee future developments, modify the division of labour and contribute to the definition of new skills. Along with teachers and researchers, and in co-operation with schools and universities, they must set up alternative arrangements that will enable young people to enter working life and retrain workers already in jobs. This means, certainly, creating 'centres of excellence' and training people in new techniques. But it also means providing those intermediate qualifications which are essential to the inner life of a company and decisive in the fight against unemployment.

All this forms part of the more general problem of education, which calls for permanent co-operation between business, school and university.

Industrial culture: post-Taylorism

An industrial culture is not shaped in a single generation. Where a tradition exists, young people and adults have within them what might be called the social chromosomes of performance.

Deindustrialization breaks up that acquisition, but it continues to underlie social life for a long time afterwards. However painful the circumstances of redeployment, it is important to preserve this potential. We ought not to deprive ourselves of the memory of the industrial past and the history of business.

The culture of trades must also change, to take account of the permanent process whereby knowledge becomes more complex, and the necessary technical specialization. The distinction between industry and services is quickly disappearing: indeed, it barely exists any longer except in official statistics. Taylorism has had its day. Dissolution of the hierarchical form, explicit co-operation between complementary individuals and teams – these are the preconditions for efficiency and quality. It has become necesssary to communicate and use a common language. It is as though the relation – fundamental to the development of humanity – between tools, techniques and language has re-emerged after decades when it was interrupted by the atomized forms of work.

Under present-day conditions of competition, valorization of business improvement and planning is being built upon this new kind of productivity. This process is not without some risk of alienation or confinement, a danger countered by workforce mobility and extended solidarities. Furthermore, the emergence of a new enterprise culture cannot take place without a reconsidered partnership, a more profound relationship between the enterprise and its environment, a revived practice of contracts negotiation.

And what about the entrepreneurial spirit? Without presenting it as a panacea, it must be said that this is of primordial importance among the ingredients of competitiveness. Does this not testify to the fact that a strong element of creativity is inherent in the new culture? Well – to say something of which everyone is only too well aware – France is short of entrepreneurs: or rather, she has been short of them for a fairly long time, extending broadly, from the end of the 1960s to the beginning of the 1980s, because there were plenty of them around at the turn of the 1950s. The children of those enterprise-creators of the immediate postwar period have devoted their youth to denouncing the consumer society and/or besieging the state machine. In an apparent paradox, it was not until the Left came into office, coinciding with the culmination of a slow process of maturation set in motion by the crisis, that minds were opened to business realities. When Raymond Barre declared, around 1980, that the unemployed had only to create their own businesses, he did little to help them do it. Since then times have changed, help has been forthcoming, and we are no longer satisfied with good or sententious words. In 1984, of 128,000 new jobs created in France, 70,000 resulted from unemployed people setting up their own companies.

They have needed courage. While public opinion today is ready to put stars of business – in the ordinary sense of the word – on the same high level as stars of show business (with as little discrimination in the one case as in the other), the financial services are in no hurry to help. The taxmen smile on creators or revivers of enterprises, but moderate their boldness in principle with timidity in action. Risk-capital companies proliferate – 170 created in three years – but many bankers still sniff at 'adventures'. As a result, the statistics list a horde of creations of individual enterprises which testify to the personal merits of their creators more than they promise any renewal of the productive fabric. And a number of truly French geniuses, after wearing themselves out in fruitless efforts in the Hexagon, have chosen the gilded exile of Silicon Valley. When we consider, further, that half of the bosses of small and medium-sized enterprises who were active at the beginning of the decade will have left the scene before its end, there are some questions to be asked.

Despite this disparity, replies come in from all over the place. The big groups are beginning to favour 'swarming' – that is, they are helping their employees to set up new enterprises, and not only in those spheres of employment where traditional heavy industry is on the downward slide. The entrepreneurial spirit is winning the day among young people and in the new professional strata. Even better, it is increasingly identified with the team spirit.

Developing and producing in order to sell

The Americans acknowledge that the chief difficulty they encounter in worldwide competition is their (at least partial) inability to transfer the results of research into the market. Whereas in most scientific areas they outwit the Japanese, on the industrial and commerical front they suffer defeat after defeat. All their efforts are concentrated on trying to overcome this handicap. Apart from the (little-known) fact that the federal state and the individual States play an essential and increasing role in study of transfers and developments, success, the best specialists tell you, depends above all on being 'market-orientated'.

Europe experiences difficulties of the same kind, often exacerbated by a feebler level of commercial dynamism. It has frequently been said that French industrial culture has been shaped by engineers rather than businessmen. This is still a problem if we consider that the expression 'market-orientated' refers to a concept that largely transcends mercantilism. It implies re-examination of all the processes, both upstream and downstream, of the act of sale in the strict sense.

True, one can sum up in the classical triptych quality/price/ delivery-date the set of questions that relate to the conditions for commercial success. To this we could add that the demands of a body of customers to whom all the world's producers address themselves are growing all the time. But meeting these demands means anticipating them – by systematic research and identifying new demands (those of enterprises served, those of individuals, those of society) and studying the responses that a product, a technology, a concept of service can offer to those demands. All this reacts back upon research and the materialization of its results, and influences the conception of products – together, of course, with their production and distribution. The organization of work and the entire field of industrial management undergo a transformation.

The increase in campaigns for quality, the concentration of all redeployment of industry on this objective, have become fashionable for the moment, and express only imperfectly the functioning of the product–market couple. What is paradoxical in this situation is that it is the commercial constraint that makes the improvement of social co-operation in business more necessary. Without that, technological process has little chance of resulting in concrete innovation.

The quality of internal management

In numerous enterprises, internal management is still archaically paternalistic or authoritarian. The demography of the employers in small and medium-sized enterprises counts a great deal here. With age, one's dynamism loses its edge; one dislikes calling on skilled advice from outside or yielding to the demands of modern management and, still more, preparing one's successors before it is too late. Among the enterprises which have suffered from the economic crisis, to the point of falling into the CIAS (*Comité Interministériel pour l'Aménagement des Structures Industrielles*), the CIRI (*Comité Interministériel de Restructuration Industrielle*) or other infirmaries, there are dozens in that situation.

Fortunately, the fabric of small and medium-sized enterprises is changing, and shock-troop enterprises are now becoming numerous, but they have not yet mastered the institutional and sociological language of their environment. And, as not all of them have access to the resources needed for competition, there is a growing chasm between those who have succeeded in crossing the threshold and the rest, who have not.

In large-scale enterprises the problem is of a different order. The positive changes observable in those small and medium-sized enterprises that are on the move take place in a relatively simple manner, owing to the proximity of the people involved. Their structures, which are slight and sometimes almost implicit, change more easily. In a big group such changes can proceed only from forms of organization, from the transmission of information, from the dissemination of an ethos and from clear-cut objectives. The success of an authentic enterprise-project – the word is more fashionable than the thing itself – depends on a will to realize it,

84

demands time, and entails putting effort into the *ad hoc* training of management and supervisors. Strategic unity and operational decentralization are both based upon communication.

Negotiating within the enterprise

At this point one cannot avoid mentioning the trade unions. All the foregoing leads to the conclusion that trade unionism must henceforth proceed along the line of constructive co-operation in ensuring the economic success of enterprises – without, however, abandoning its task of fighting to defend the workers. This twofold commitment could be the basis for new compromises.

One might as well say at once that this is not going to happen automatically. As an institution as well as a social movement, trade unionism is the ambiguous outcome of a history which has shaped its culture at the same time as the form of the wage relation and collective guarantees. In the present context of economic competition, a certain number of established facts – social, legal or contractual – are ceasing to be appropriate. Some of them constitute brakes on progress and, in particular, worsen the division between those who have a steady job and the various groups lying outside that category. The way those workers who have fallen victim to the abolition of their jobs are treated varies according to all sorts of factors. The tradition of a business that finds itself in difficulties and the symbolic significance associated with its sector of activity give rise to a greater or lesser degree of mobilization by the forces of trade unionism. The public authorities show a greater or lesser degree of voluntarism. The compensation obtained by workers also depends on their previous gains whose extent, naturally, is commensurate with the importance of the enterprise.

Flexibility, too, comes up against various established facts. It has to find compensations in rearrangement of the length of the working day, in the autonomy and responsibility of individuals and teams, in training schemes that result in a real qualification and career prospects, in clearer information regarding decisions, in the opportunity to discuss options which have implications for the future. All these aspects are interlinked and this means, in every significant case, that overall negotiation and compromise are required.

In this respect the trade unions, French and European alike, searching for an identity. If they are to go enthusiastically down that road, they must find attentive and resolute representatives both among individual heads of businesses and in the body of employers as an institution. For the moment, the employers' talk about modernization is exclusively emphasizing adaptation to the new conditions of competition. This is no guarantee of social dialogue. The first task of the politician, in the domain of labour relations, is to busy himself with getting these contractual adjustments recognized as valid and effective. This can give rise to a 'political exchange' which will include reciprocal and lasting legitimation of representatives.

Participation rights are better than shareholding

Popular shareholding, warhorse of the late Chirac government and 'moral' justification for its privatizations, means barely more than supplementing the pay of the workforce. As such, its financial attractiveness is understandable. True, it is accompanied by a policy of developing 'quality circles', an interesting initiative in relation to competitiveness but one about which it is rather difficult to say whether, in practice, it offers every possible opportunity for worker initiative. Sometimes it even serves merely to short-circuit the role of the trade unions and the workers' elected representatives.

Participation is conceivable only with partners who are free and in possession of acknowledged rights. If the needs of the age are to be met, participation must allow workers to intervene effectively in the organization and content of their work, and also to give their views on certain aspects of the enterprise's strategic choices. This means that forms of direct participation must be embraced within a general conception of social relations that includes the expression of conflicts, negotiation and sharing of initiative on the organization of work, the quality of products, and management itself.

Such a conception must be based on a harmonizing of the old and new rights of the employees, and must allow for various forms of representation. The economic role played by enterprise committees has increased and will continue to increase: this is the surest way to prevent them from being reduced merely to organizing leisure activities and distributing Christmas presents to the workers' children. The experience of having elected workforce representatives on the boards of national enterprises is too recent and, at the moment, too limited for any conclusions to be drawn. Yet it has begun to provide proof that the workforce administrators were capable of discussing the strategy of an enterprise, even of deciding it in an appropriate way. But transposing this arrangement to the private sector creates problems. Nevertheless, this trail deserves to be followed more thoroughly than is provided for in the timid section dealing with it in the 1986 law on privatization, if only to bring together the different national experiences within Europe.

Wider solidarities for employment

Three lines of thought open up before the trade-union world, lines of unequal difficulty: solidarity between workers and unemployed for increasing and improving employment; developing trade unionism in small and medium-sized enterprises; linking up the sphere of work with life outside it. They could be explored concretely on the basis of decentralized negotiation at enterprise or local level. While it is obvious that this will not, by itself, solve the problem of unemployment, its dynamic may be able to make a contribution. We see this clearly when trade unions and business heads get together in local initiatives for development: when that happens, it gives a different consistency to economic activity. In the same way, we can think of many forms of co-operation between industry and the universities resulting from a pragmatic approach.

Where contract negotiation is concerned, we must not give up innovation as a lost cause – contrary to what one might believe from a superficial reading of social life in France. Almost everywhere in Europe new developments are taking shape: agreements on training and employment, on the introduction of new technology, on rearrangement of working hours, on productivity, on consultation; agreements concluded at the level of the company, the trade, the country and even the Community. The governments and partners in the European social dialogue have identified a minimum basis of guarantees and have thereby created the conditions for negotiating an all-European harmonization. This presupposes convergence by the trade unions towards a priority objective – namely, employment – along certain fundamental axes:

- flexibility in production in exchange for a substantial reduction in the length of the working day (an idea put forward by the German metalworkers);
- concentration of resources on training young people and their absorption into jobs, and on retraining workers who have been made redundant;
- transition from the black economy and social protection to recognized jobs which satisfy a new demand.

Towards trade-union renewal

Extending worker solidarity beyond the interests they share through being employed in the same company or the same branch of industry – this is, by definition, the role of the trade unions.

Throughout its history, trade unionism has been concerned to promote the progress of society as a whole. In practice it has promoted, successively, two forms of solidarity. In the early days of industrialization, the trade unions of the skilled workers were able to bring their labour market under effective control. In the age of Ford and Keynes, industrial trade unionism succeeded in extending worker solidarity to the employed class as a whole, by way of wage scales and social protection. By joining in the

Fordist compromise,[1] however, it gave up the small degree of control over production that skilled workers had been able to acquire during the previous period. It has never wholly recovered that ground.

After May 1968, however, the preconditions for a renewal of the trade unions began to appear. Shaken by a salutary electric shock, the employers modernized themselves. Contract negotiation took place in an atmosphere of ostentatious display. Large-scale agreements on employment and training gave grounds for looking forward to a fruitful future. The crisis sharply interrupted that process. After a time, the trade unions succeeded in grasping the gravity of the situation. However, they completely underestimated the capacity for 'forward flight' possessed by worldwide capitalism. In the face of the looming dangers their first reaction was defensive, and they were unable to find a new dynamic. On the employers' side, rejection of constraints and burdens took precedence over a search for negotiated compromise, and this was all the easier for them because the rise in unemployment weakened worker solidarity.

So far as their effects can be gauged, the Auroux Acts of 1982 failed to deal with trade-union difficulties. Most of the Left, convinced that to understand trade unionists it is enough to have matey conversations with them, have not yet recovered. Now, however, the problem largely transcends the French situation. It is European, even global. We need to step out of the logic of easy growth and centralized regulation on the national level, which was what determined the whole system of collective guarantees. We need to smash the Fordist compromise. Without making a clean sweep of the past, these reconsiderations are needed if we are to construct a new covenant of solidarity among all categories, both old and new, of employed and unemployed, and to define the mutual concessions appropriate to the new worldwide economic deal.

Europe demands this renewal, and at the same time offers the opportunity for it. Today, for example, we see the trade unions of Germany and Italy, formerly so different, developing convergent ideas and experiences. On the microeconomic level, progress in decentralized negotiation has been necessary, if not sufficient, for the renewal of forms of social protection and the emergence of a new industrial compromise, for both necessitate a more direct individual in initiative and solidarity. There is an imperative here that must tend to favour renewal of trade unionism from below, as a social movement and as an institution. The trade unions, for their part, need to revive their links with their members at every level, to direct their efforts towards the training of their activists and, in some cases, to establish greater coherence between everyday experience and what is said at headquarters. And to get the best out of all these new experiences, many meetings will be needed, and much thought and research at local, trade, national and European level.

It remains true that such an immense recomposition enterprise will fail in its objectives if trade-union action does not secure results. For this, three participants are needed: the trade unions, the employers, and the state. The government's will to promote the emergence of a new negotiated compromise ought to be given stronger expression. As for the employers, whose extreme heterogeneity should not be forgotten, the least one can say is that all their representatives do not venture with the same zeal upon the path of renewal. Their most modernistic advances do not guarantee that they will opt for an active development of contract policy. That will recover its full vigour only if society as a whole recognizes its politicocultural necessity. But is this not a theme that can win a comfortable majority in the world of ideas?

TWELVE

We Must Not Resign Ourselves to Unemployment

IMBALANCES AND TRANSFORMATIONS IN THE LABOUR MARKET

S INCE the first oil shock we have seen both a sharp rise in unemployment and a profound transformation of the way the labour market functions. As a result of these developments there has been an explosion in the employment and unemployment situation, and in costs to France's economy and society, which justify our refusal to resign ourselves to permanent underemployment – especially as some countries have managed to find answers to the challenge of unemployment.

The rise in unemployment

At the end of 1987 there were 2,600,000 unemployed. The rate of unemployment, less than 2 per cent at the beginning of the 1960s, increased sharply thereafter and went on increasing until, in mid 1988, it embraced 11 per cent of the active population.

This increase has been a matter of simple arithmetic: the resources of labour-power and the demand for jobs increase, the supply of jobs wavers, the number of available jobs declines. Two contradictory logics of adaptation are at work. For the workers, the factors causing increased demand for work remain the same. The demographic effect of the 'baby boom' persists and women's entry into the labour market has not decreased during the recession, contrary to what happened in the past. Since 1975 the active population has grown each year by 0.8 per cent, or 190,000 people. This tendency will continue until the end of the century, even if it does diminish progressively. Only after 2005 should resources of labour-power start to decline.

For business, on the contrary, 1974 really was a turning point. In the first place, the increase in the supply of jobs slowed markedly. Then, after the second oil shock, a reduction in the numbers employed began. From then on, employment fell in both industry and agriculture, and the service sector became a less dynamic employer. Altogether, an average of 40,000 jobs disappeared every year. This situation was not due solely to the slowdown in economic activity. The operating conditions of the production process were changing, with industrial restructurings and investments that favoured rationalization of production processes rather than increased capacity. The substitution of capital for labour was proceeding more rapidly, and labour productivity was growing faster than production. This development bore down hard on employment and conveyed a feeling – more subjective than real – that labour was progressively becoming a more or less fixed factor in production, a decision to hire being regarded as difficult to reverse. The supply of jobs was inadequate for the new demand.

If policy does not change, this will go on until the end of the century. Under these conditions the persistence of high rates of unemployment seems, in the short term, to be a fairly universal phenomenon in the industrialized countries, among which France cuts a particulary poor figure.

In the midterm, however, there is a possibility that situations between the different countries will diverge markedly. This can be measured through the effort to increase employment which would be needed to bring the rate of unemployment back to its 1979 level by 1995.[1] In the United States and Japan it would be enough to maintain the rate of growth observed between 1979 and 1985. In the Federal Republic of Germany the employed population would have to be reduced by no more than half a per cent per year. In France, on the contrary, employment would need to be increased by 1.2 per cent per year, whereas it has been falling by 0.4 per cent since 1979. We have here a potent factor of disparity in the constraints that will bear upon economic policies, and reduced encouragement to make them converge.

Transformations in the labour market

The increase in the number of people seeking employment reflects a profound imbalance in the labour market, but this depressed situation should not be seen as a freeze-up. The most conspicuous sign that this is not so is the large-scale movement of labour which is profoundly affecting the way human resources are allocated, but is concealed by the measurement of it given by the net variations in numbers employed. If, between 1978 and 1984, the number of jobs filled fell annually by half a per cent, that resulted from a rotation of nearly a quarter of the employed population, or a yearly displacement of labour involving about five million people.

This labour-market vitality has its source in profound changes. Businesses have adapted themselves to the transformations in a fluctuating economic and institutional environment. Forms of labour management have become complex and diverse. Employment is less and less a homogenous category. The traditional norms of waged work, based on a labour contract that includes no time limit and offers more or less upward-moving careers, is on the way out. Atypical forms of employment are becoming frequent, intermediate situations are emerging, and vague and porous boundaries now separate inactivity, employment and unemployment.

The themes of flexibility and work-sharing which crystallized –

somewhat negatively – the social debate in the 1980s have largely become reality under business pressure, and have been facilitated by public policy. Adjustment of labour costs has become easier. Large-scale unemployment, reduced unemployment pay, rethinking about indexation, and increasing individualization of wage policies provide a setting that is conducive to flexibility in wage costs.

We can also observe a transformation in the status of the employed population. The 'hard core' corresponding to the traditional norm of the wage-earning class continues to form the majority, in France as in the other industrialized countries. According to the statisticians, a person who has a 'normal' job can expect to hold it down for twenty-three years in Japan, seventeen years in most of the European countries, and fourteen years in North America.

This hard core is crumbling as a result of a combination of several factors. The restructuring of the traditional branches of industry is bringing face to face with unemployment a large number of workers who used to be sheltered from it. Legislation has provided a framework for diversifying status and, since 1986, has moved towards weakening the protection of both individual and collective employment. And the existence and development of thresholds in social legislation restrict the degree of protection provided in small and medium-sized enterprises just when the total employment share of these enterprises is increasing in France. The image of a comet seems a good metaphor for the employment system. This star consists of a nucleus which shrinks and a tail which expands. The halo is formed by a workforce which is peripheral, marginal and underemployed.

The peripheral element can escape the constraints of the norm for workers, and it has increased steadily since 1976, with a substantial growth of insecure situations: temporary, fixed-term contracts. . . . In 1986 half a million people, or 3 per cent of workers, were in this category. But this factor plays a major role in the movement of labour, because in 1986 70 per cent of recruitment was made on the basis of an insecure contract. The marginal element is the labour which hovers on the border between activity, unemployment and training. This results from the different forms in which unemployment is treated socially, together with the different ways of integrating young people into the world of work – apprenticeships, day-release schemes and other kinds of training. This element is as significant as the peripheral element. Underemployed labour means those workers who, working less than is normal or usual for them, are looking for another job. This group embraces a further half-million people and is increasing rapidly (it has doubled in the last four years). Altogether, one worker in ten is outside the hard core of the active population, and is suffering the fits and starts of the crisis and its negative effects. If we add the unemployed to this total, we account for 20 per cent of the active population.

THE DAMAGING EFFECTS OF UNEMPLOYMENT

Unemployment, like employment, has become fragmented. It extends, spreads, attacks an increasing number of social strata, and becomes more and more unequal in its effects.

The observable structures of unemployment are very unbalanced. They include more young people, underskilled women and people with a low level of training. When several of these criteria coincide, some dramatic figures result. Twenty-six per cent of active women under twenty are unemployed. Forty per cent of young people are unemployed when they leave school. One could go on categorizing these victims of disasters; one could compile league tables; but it is more useful to identify the dynamic that underlies these imbalances.

Four aspects are immediately obvious. The unemployment that takes the form of inability to enter the world of work affects school leavers and women who are trying to return to work. The level of qualification possessed or acquired constitutes the strongest protection against this type of unemployment. Repeated unemployment results from the development of insecure forms of employment. A quarter of the unemployed are in that situation at the end of a temporary job or a fixed-term contract. This affects mainly young people and women, but is tending to spread among other categories as well. Redeployment affects adults in the traditional industries who have lost their jobs as a result of industrial restructuring. Finally, unemployment by exclusion, which originally affected mainly older workers over fifty or the disabled, has spread to other groups through the growth of early retirement.

Naturally, these categories overlap, but most importantly they are beginning to form a pattern, with paths of exclusion which carry unemployed people who are in the process of redeployment or initiation towards long-term unemployment, via insecure jobs which succeed one another at longer and longer intervals.

Exclusion means, first of all, long-term unemployment. In 1986 the average period of unemployment was 15.7 months, as against eight months in 1974. This means that the average unemployed person in France is in a state of long-term unemployment. A quarter of our unemployed have been out of a job for more than two years. The phenomenon no longer affects the elderly alone, but also men and women in the prime of life (54 per cent) and young people (20 per cent).

This long-term unemployment, the source of a social exclusion which is sometimes irreversible, has several causes. The first is failure to adapt to an age of rapid technological change. Qualifications and skills do not match the needs of employers who have profited from the crisis to raise their demands. Unqualified or older workers are particularly vulnerable at the present time.

The second cause relates to the phenomenon of the queue in a stagnant labour market. At any given moment, a certain number of people are losing their jobs. Those who are best qualified, those who offer the greatest productive potential, will find work within a few months. Those who have not found it by then will have to face competition from more recent recruits to the ranks of the unemployed, some of whom possess, in their turn, attributes that will enable them to go to the front of the queue for jobs. In consequence, the less competitive among the unemployed find themselves pushed further and further back in the queue and plunged deeper and deeper into long-term unemployment.

Finally, there is the phenomenon of rejection. The situation of the long-term unemployed is made worse by the fact that they are often spurned by employers merely because they have been out of work for a long time. In the first place, the fact that someone has been unemployed for a long time indicates to a potential employer that he has probably been turned down already by several other employers. Secondly, prolonged absence from activity is hardly conducive to productivity when a person gets back into work. Knowledge and skills have deteriorated; working habits have become rusty; and for many the experience of long-term unemployment can have serious psychological and even physiological effects.

In general, long-term unemployment operates like a sort of trap: the longer an unemployed person is caught in it, the longer they will have to wait before they can hope to get another job.

The costs of unemployment

Budget reductions, cuts in social expenditure, savage restructuring – everything is permitted in order to come into line with current taste, rather as though the number of people cast aside by the labour market ensured one a certificate of good economic management. Yet rigour cannot be a one-way affair. Unemployment is not economically and financially neutral – it causes severe rents in the social fabric and deeply wounds those who remain in it for a long time.

The *economic* costs of unemployment are the losses in production, together with the degradation of skills and human capital which results from the non-utilization of labour. Those costs are static – the loss of production is suffered in one go – but also dynamic, for unemployment reduces incomes, and consequently the propensity to spend, the demand for goods, and eventually (subject to the balance of trade) production itself.

The *financial* costs include the expense of unemployment pay and an employment policy, together with the loss in tax receipts and social security payments. Experts estimated that in 1983 these financial costs represented 6.5 per cent of the Gross National Product, or 259 billion francs. Unemployment therefore exerts what economists call a scissors effect, since it both increases expenditure and reduces receipts, by narrowing the basis for contributions.

The social costs cannot be overlooked. In the first place there is poverty, the return of '*les misérables*'. The individual effects are less quantifiable but just as distressing. In a society in which one's occupation dominates one's social relations, in an urban society which has broken with the traditional forms of solidarity, unemployment causes social mutilation, because it entails loss of status. The unemployed person falls abruptly from a society of time-consuming work into empty time filled only by idleness, anxiety and shame. How many unemployed people even try to fool those around them that they are going off to work every morning? Yet this overwhelming reality must not cause us to forget that there is a wide variation in reactions and several different factors to consider:

> The most important is probably the individual's professional and cultural heritage. This determines his capacity to respond and the way he responds to the initial trauma, together with the kind of defences he can put up and the alternative plans he can devise. From this point of view, unemployment amplifies inequality. As a general rule, the unemployed person resists better the higher his level of training and qualifications, and also if he enjoys close-knit family and social relations and can set some mechanisms of solidarity in motion.[2]

Even so, however, the longer unemployment lasts, the capacity to resist diminishes. Irreversible changes can result.

Attention must be drawn – albeit with care – to a serious social phenomenon. Suicide has become much more common since 1976 (by 40 per cent) and was the cause of 12,000 deaths in 1982, about the same number as road accidents. Suicide is an individual drama and to account for it, mechanically, by unemployment would not be honest. Yet statistical experience and sociology tell us that

The suicide rate is a social indicator which is particularly sensitive to the nature of the relations prevailing among members of a social group or a society. The stronger the factors of cohesion and integration, the fewer the suicides, and vice versa. The increase in suicides in the last ten years in France is related, therefore, to a dilapidation or weakening of the elements of cohesion and integration in our society.[3]

And it is hard to deny that unemployment has made a considerable contribution to that process.

THE PRICE OF EXCELLENCE IN EMPLOYMENT

We must not resign ourselves to unemployment and under-employment, and we can derive some hope from the fact that there are countries which have succeeded in keeping to or attaining relatively low unemployment levels. This 'excellence' is costly to them, certainly, but we should consider its limits and its price.

Several countries have lessons to teach us: Sweden, Norway, Austria, but also the United States, have succeeded in stemming or restricting the rise in unemployment. The Europeans and the Americans have followed very different routes to achieve different results. For this reason we shall distinguish between two models, according to the effectiveness of the formula applied.

Thanks to the fresh look at our old continent taken by two Canadians,[4] we can see how original is a European model of full or almost full employment, with an unemployment rate not exceeding 3 per cent. In the policies of Norway, Sweden and Austria we can find grounds for rejecting pessimism and also guidelines for reversing the depressing trends which dominate the labour markets of the industrialized countries.

These countries have not invented a magic formula. Depending on region and period, the efficacity of their policies is due to a coherent group of measures which are in harmony with their institutions and culture and evolve with the economic environment. In countries that are wide open to the outside world, the objective of full employment cannot be attained by disregarding inflation and the need for a balance in public expenditure.

The vitality of the American economy acquires its full significance at the microeconomic and decentralized level. A State-by-State and region-by-region analysis brings out the crucial role of the actors and their setting. We find ourselves looking at a Schumperterian model of development, in which the synergy between creators of enterprises, local employment authorities and the banking system is fully operational. Its originality lies in the recent and massive development of a partnership between three components: universities, local communities and business. This very flexible, only slightly institutionalized association is focused on concrete projects and shows a strong will to bring them to fruition.

THIRTEEN

A Different Way of Living and Working

I T MAY seem presumptuous to try to distinguish some lines of force for future ways of life and work when socioeconomic development is tainted with so many intersecting and overlapping uncertainties, discontinuities and innovations, and finding a vision for the future is hampered by the fact that there are as many uncertainties as there are ups and downs.

This lack of visibility increases one's pessimism about employment. Fifteen years of irresistible and large-scale rise in unemployment, in a context of slowed-down growth, will not be easily wiped out either in statistics or in men's minds: especially as even if we find a more satisfactory path of growth, and even if employment policies become more effective, this will not be enough to bring back *full* employment.

Nevertheless, we should not succumb to resignation. An obstacle can be useful for progress, as Jean Monnet pointed out. Even unemployment can be creative. As an obstacle, as a heavy liability for the future, and as wastage, its grip on the economy and society compels us to seek unorthodox solutions. Neither a utopian return to the growth model of the 'golden sixties' nor a new golden age of liberalism seems a credible response. Our model of development is

101

now out of breath; the forms of regulation which favoured it are exhausted.

Hence, then, the interest being taken in new ways of organizing activity which may cure the imbalances and exclusions, through greater diversity of lifestyle and economic and social regulation. If we study changes in and prospects for ways of life and work, we could succeed in discovering new paths.

From dysfunction to a change of values

The disruption of the old order outlines the potential for a different development. The tensions resulting from the massive scale of economic and social processes cause irregularities and frustration. Standardized mass production, based on a Taylorist organization of work, has reached the limits of its effectiveness. A source of social costs, it is too rigid to respond to differentiated demands and concern for quality in products and management. Furthermore, it imprisoned the workers in the rigid framework of the production clock. Mass consumption does not go well with an evolution of ways of life and values which entails on the contrary, a search for differentiation and personalization in services rendered, and also in goods to be consumed.

The welfare state is suffering, as Habermas puts it, from a crisis of legitimation. The phenomena of counterproductiveness, of 'nemesis', already invoked by Ivan Illich seem to be spreading. More medical treatment is not a pledge of better health, and compulsory and lengthened school attendance has not lowered the level of illiteracy. Collective functions are being called into question, while their costs seem hard to bear. Social protection is a fair example. It seems too costly for the available resources, yet leaves entire categories of the population uncovered, despite its aim to be all-embracing. And it provides services that are too anonymous and uniform, failing to respond to the growing diversity of situations, aspirations and needs.

Gigantism and its dysfunctionings are not unconnected with the sort of centrifugal movement of values which is affecting French society, causing sociological fragmentation and fluidity of ideological loyalties. Through opinion polls and work on 'the lifestyles of the French' we can observe the forms of cultural multi-membership which are breaking up the classical structures. Writings on electoral behaviour reveal a great deal of instability in political choices. The citizens – or at least some of them – are becoming more and more individualistic, freeing themselves from religious, occupational and social doctrines, and the electorate is becoming more and more volatile.

In the social field of aspirations we can observe movements which are at first sight discordant. An abundance of initiatives, original approaches and innovations seek to find expression in the world of commerce. The renewal of entrepreneurship corresponds to a will to win independence from the state and to realize oneself within small-scale social frameworks. This promotion of enterprise goes far beyond the economic sphere. The spirit of innovation is not incompatible with paying attention to certain forms of collective interest – an alternative model of work and authority, a different way of using the human factor, mobilization of energies for the benefit of local development. This 'sixty-eight-ist' capitalism[1] harmonizes with the new paradigm of performance and competitiveness in firms which give priority to motivation, involvement, human-scale units of production and wide dissemination of information.

What a strange and stimulating paradox is this hybrid encounter between the margin and the heart of society, converging towards the valorization of profit and conviviality! The fact that the Left is in power is not unconnected with this invigorating mixture. Solidarity, too, is changing. It is evolving more and more towards a moral militancy, a spirit of resistance to unacceptable situations – violation of human rights, poverty, and unemployment too. Faced with underemployment, civil society is inventing new values and new technologies. Inspired by the pragmatic formulas of Amnesty International, movements are trying to find concrete, immediate answers to social exclusion and mutilation. This is the function of 'New Solidarities Against Unemployment'.

This association, created in 1985, is experimenting with a

simple, new formula for job creation and help for people who are trying to get back into society. Volunteers organized in solidarity groups pool some of their income to finance jobs created for the unemployed to match their specific abilities. These jobs consist of work intended to help other victims of exclusion. They provide opportunities for relationships of friendship and mutual aid which are as personalized as possible. The money collected is used to hire unemployed people, on a part-time basis and for six-month periods (one has to have worked for 507 hours in the previous six months if one is to claim unemployment pay). The people so hired are placed, according to their abilities, at the disposal of large or voluntary groups, so that they may contribute to the development of these bodies.

This temporary work contract gives an opportunity to establish a personal, all-round relationship with someone who is in danger of being excluded from society. Personal, in that the individual being helped is supported by at least two members of the solidarity group who, in a bond of mutual trust, help them to emerge from their loneliness, to get back into the saddle, to get used to the constraints of work at their trade once more and, at the end of the six months, to make a start at re-entry into the world of work. All-round, because unemployed people frequently suffer from a series of disadvantages which are mutually reinforcing and which one has to try to reduce simultaneously. We can see that while money is precious, availability is no less so: both are indispensable.

Civil society is not resigning itself to underemployment. Ingenious 'do-it-yourself' schemes increase, in a kaleidoscopic mosaic of pragmatic responses to concrete situations of unemployment and exclusion.[2]

Maps of the future

Recognizing which trends are significant, and fixing the socio-economic changes in a long-term context, will save us from being misled by ephemera, by the foam of innovation which can conceal radical movement. To draw a map may nevertheless seem an audacious and difficult undertaking in so uncertain a situation. Staying with the analogy of cartography, our representation of the future can be made only in broad terms, defining outlines, as in the old navigators' maps that showed a succession of ports and coasts – what were called 'portolans'.[3] Three anchorage points can be sketched in.

First, the ascendancy of demography – what Fernand Braudel calls the weight of the number, that 'excellent indicator of the decisive relations between the human masses'. And these masses are going to balance out differently, according to age, family relations and activity, the flows of population and employment at the dawn of the third millennium.

The 'grandad boom' will constitute, as the second millennium draws to its close, an exact mirror-image of the baby boom. Low birth rates and lengthened life expectancy will contribute to an ageing population.

The proportion of adults (in the sense of people between adolescence and old age) will stabilize at slightly over 50 per cent, while there will be a change over in the proportion of young people and elderly people in the active population. The ageing of the population which is already apparent can be illustrated by these figures: in 2005, 21 per cent of the population will be over sixty and 8 per cent over seventy-five (as against 4 per cent in 1960). Social systems as they function at present will be profoundly affected, in so far as the elderly are recipients of services and social payments partly supplied by the state. Social security tends to overdoctor old people: this is an ethical problem, certainly, but also a financial one.

The OECD forecasts that between now and 2040 in the seven principal industrialized countries, ageing is likely to augment the total cost of social programmes, by a third in real terms, by doubling the cost of retirement pensions and increasing expenditure on health by 40 per cent. Everywhere, eventually, this question will be asked: Can our ageing population be coped with in a way that is both more satisfactory to them and less expensive for the community? Hospitalizing the average insured person during the last three weeks of their life costs the community as much as all the hospitalization they receive in their life up to that time.

Household composition has already been altered by a reduction in the importance of the traditional family. There will be more households, because there will be fewer people in each unit. Individuals living alone or in couples will predominate, while one-parent families will continue to increase significantly. There will be a greater variety of household types, owing to the fragility and instability of family structures. This structural evolution has its source in a diversification of individual life cycles, which are less uniform, more unstable; and also in a tendency towards individualization and autonomy. From this result, too, an increasing precariousness in economic situations and an increasing amount of solitude in society. Here also, important new needs are appearing: housing, food, sociability, leisure, transport . . .

Women's economic activity should continue to progress. In this sphere the difference from other industrialized countries is symptomatic of the possible limits. In less than ten years the rate of women's economic activity has increased by ten points in the United States, as against only four in France. This progress amounts to a 'quiet revolution', with women becoming aware of a need to break with their traditional image and place in society. It is independent neither of the threats to employment nor of the instability of couples, which entail, either from necessity or as a precaution, an ever-greater scale of entry into the labour market, despite unemployment. The need for child-minders, home helps, catering, specific provision for leisure and holidays, is therefore going to increase, changing all the while. We ought to see this evolution not as a constraint but as an opportunity. The female labour force will still, however, encounter difficulty in acquiring qualifications, and will have to accept, for lack of anything better at present, jobs which are less well paid and more flexible than others.

Our age is at a crossroads of ways of life and work. The dialectic of the pace of life and of activity in occupations deeply affects the economic and social prospects before us. The balance between time under constraint and free time is one important dimension of this.

Some original data[4] illuminate in a new way the trends in use of work time. The total time spent at work by the nation, which remained steady during the 'thirty glorious years' at around forty-one billion hours per year, underwent a marked decline between 1974 and 1984. Fewer people were now working, and for shorter periods: there had been rearrangements of and reductions in working hours, and a fifth week's paid holiday had become general. The result was a five-billion-hour decrease in working hours, four of them since 1978. Free time increased by twenty-two billion hours between 1974 and 1984, with nearly half of it devoted to holidays and watching television.

Time under constraint,[5] having been considerably surpassed by free time, has ceased to dominate people's balance of time. One comparison gives cause for thought: in 1984 Frenchmen over the age of fifteen spent, altogether, more hours watching television than working. On an individual level, the life cycle has been profoundly altered. In 1946 a worker aged twenty had the prospect of spending, on average, one-third of his waking life at work; by 1975 only a quarter; and today less than a fifth. These changes, recent but profound, are likely to continue and to induce other logics of production and exchange.

Free time can become a factor in the development of new activities – leisure, tourism, various services, and new jobs. The forms of 'self-production' which never disappeared – DIY, gardening, knitting – should find fresh fields of application. Some might see this as social archaism, but it also means that a new balance between market and non-market economies is beginning to emerge. What better proof of this potential is there than the commercial strategy of industrialists, large-scale distributors or advertisers who are offering furniture or pictures in kit form and leaving completion of individual houses to their buyers? A barter economy may also develop,[6] in which abilities will be exchanged through intermediaries or quasi-markets. The effects of all this on employment are ambivalent. The self-service economy can abolish jobs: 10,000 jobs have vanished from France's service stations. But by making acceptable, or even attractive, reductions in working hours which are not fully compensated, 'self-production' contributes to the creation of lasting jobs.

Choices between income and free time have changed, however. In the EC, in France, the trend which advocated sharing of work and income has ceased to predominate. Aspirations regarding time and income are more various, so that internal flexibility and shortening of working hours can be balanced, negotiated and exchanged.

The driving forces of demand

Three out of four of the goods and services which will be consumed in the year 2000 do not exist at present. Now, there is still a brake on the development of certain new activities and therefore of employment: this is due mainly to persistent failure to adapt supply to the demand for services and goods whose potential, in activity and job creation, remains unexploited. There are activities, now neglected, which can become sources of employment. We have to reverse Say's law of markets: demand can create supply, in a complex alchemy which transforms into jobs a demand which has been left uncultivated, as the CFDT[7] has clearly perceived:

> Running ahead of new demand means placing waymarks for a new model of growth which will be less homogeneous, more diversified, leaving more room for social innovation, initiative and decentralization of authority. It is our ambition to contribute responses that are better adapted to needs, without thereby sinking into a kind of dual society.

This is an approach to development which should be tried. It seeks to bring about convergence between the search for alternatives to the classical forms of supply and the impulses that result from potential demand.

Development will then recover its original dimension as an overall project, both economic and social. *Economic*, in that what matters is not so much to 'find optimal combinations of resources and factors of production as to bring to light and mobilize resources and capacities that are hidden, scattered or wrongly used . . . in energy, capital and entrepreneurial spirit'.[8] *Social* – a vision dear to Alain Touraine, who sees development as transition from one level of society's intervention in itself to another, higher level, combining new investments with extended forms of social participation.[9]

Without claiming to exhaust the subject, we can illustrate this approach, which aims at transforming potentials into activities.

The increase in free time engenders demands – for leisure, and for new activities which can often be paid for. The non-profit-making voluntary sector doubled the number of its workers employed in recreational, cultural and sporting services between 1980 and 1986. As a result of involving their supporters and making good use of their shared equipment, these voluntary organizations succeeded in transforming emergent demands into paying activities, and doing so in competition with both private and public sectors.

The culture industry is rich in potential. The source of 770,000 jobs, it will experience between now and the year 2000[10] an annual 4 per cent increase in demand. Every household will devote twice as much to it as it spends on clothing: 10 per cent of its budget, as opposed to 5 per cent at the end of the 1960s. Take music, for example: there is a growing interest in both listening and performing. The revival of musical life in France has been recognized by all observers. It affects all forms of music and finds expression in the development of active listening. There has been talk of an 'explosion' in music festivals, but this applies also to performing, both individual and collective. Demand for instruction continues to be unsatisfied, if we are to judge by the waiting list in most conservatoires and schools of music. Answers have been found.

For instance, in one rural community a music workshop was set up in 1979 on the initiative of families who wished their children to have a musical education. Their initial aim was entertainment and teaching music. The numbers attending increased rapidly: twenty pupils in 1979, four hundred in 1983, six hundred and fifty in 1985. The workshop employed thirty people, mostly as part-time teachers. Funding is assured by the parents, through a subscription of four hundred to five hundred francs per term.

As for housing, health, childminding, care of certain categories of the disabled, and aid and home help for the aged, the traditional policies are incapable of coping with the diversity of people's situations and the resulting diversity of demands. Here, too, the voluntary sector has proved its dynamism – admittedly, under the aegis of the welfare state, and thanks to its financial backing. In the sphere of social action (the disabled, the aged, home helps, crèches and short-stay day nurseries) the numbers of paid staff increased by 75 per cent between 1980 and 1986.[11] There is considerable potential for development, because demand in this sphere is so far from being satisfied, and not always due to lack of money.

Take childminding. It is calculated that 2.3 million children under the age of three are involved, a million of them with mothers out at work. Of this million, only 400,000 are in crèches, day nurseries or nursery schools. The existing supply does not correspond to need, either in quantity or, in some cases, in quality. And there are parents who could pay for this service even if they are not both working.

The potential market for childminding should not, therefore, be confined to the million children under the age of three whose mothers are out at work. Although it would be foolhardy to give an estimate of the total potential demand, it probably covers several thousand children. To give an idea of what is involved in terms of direct employment, we may consider that an additional supply of 100,000 full-time childminding units (about twenty days per month) would correspond, in terms of collective crèches, to the creation of between 20,000 and 30,000 new jobs.

Many more areas and examples could be given in illustration of this approach to the problem. On the basis of a potential demand, a process of activity creation is promoted. For this purpose a specific mobilization of resources and a flexible utilization of human resources and capacities should be co-ordinated.

The finance and resources needed for this development can be very diverse. In the first place, a large part of the demand is self-sustainable, since many people are ready to pay for goods and services hitherto unavailable. Moreover, these activities can glean the funds required through a less costly way of meeting social demands, childminding and home help . . .

Another example of a more economic management of social expenditure would be a different way of using unemployment pay, to transform passive expenditure into active aid towards job creation.

FOURTEEN

Competitiveness and Solidarity

THE purpose of this book is to find a path for France which will be both practical and ambitious – without in any way overlooking the constraints imposed by the world as it is, but looking at this world as it changes. Opening one's eyes to the world compels recognition both of the difficulties – often serious – and the real opportunities that face us. One thing is certain: no economic health or social dynamism is possible without competitiveness. The increase in worldwide interdependence and the limits of national resources lead us to resituate this requirement within the wider setting of a pan–European plan. The history of the state in France and comparison of this history with other experiences enable us to put forward a new view of our state's relations with society. Moreover, in business present circumstances provide a real opportunity for the world of labour, on condition that education valorizes the knowledge which that world possesses, renews and nurtures it. But this opportunity can be grasped only by people who are in work, and given prospects that favour their continued employment.

Now, our idea is not just to exalt the economic performance of business in the face of competition, still less to exalt aggressiveness in a pitiless world. It is to create, for everyone living in our country the conditions for a better life, both individual and social. This is the necessary basis for all progress and all change. This is the fundamental reason why we cannot resign ourselves to unemployment. We must overcome the weaknesses of the social protection system and seek active ways of responding to new needs. More generally, we have to construct a new relationship between competitiveness and solidarity. The prospect of a different way of living and working has already been realized in a number of experiments. However, the dynamism of the voluntary sector cannot by itself pull everything towards a new model of development – we must define an approach with a more general bearing. And before we come to deciding on concrete directions for action, we must stand back and check on difficulties and experiences on a global scale, understand what is at stake, and choose a long-term strategy.

General worldwide difficulties

The republican state, the economy, education, unemployment, even the new experiences – all have very specific features in France. But we cannot close our eyes to the fact that developed nations everywhere, with unequal levels of well-being, are trying to solve the same problems. Because interdependence is increasing in the world economy, the same phenomena are appearing everywhere. More essentially, though, how can one not see that we are living through a time of change? And if values themselves seem to be shaken, is this not because the age-old recipes which made them so significant in social life have become inadequate?

Are economic dynamism and social cohesion incompatible? Under present conditions one would be tempted to answer: not in principle but yes, alas, in practice. Modernization does away with jobs. The intelligence revolution creates few jobs and, on the contrary, causes redundancies. Social protection extends, becomes a heavier burden, leaves gaps, and poverty re-emerges.

We have just seen that the actual movement of society and the experiences that arise from this movement reveal hitherto unsuspected possibilities, and open a way for social forms which were previously utopian. But the possible response to new needs is neither spontaneous nor easy to formulate, and the richest experiences are developing at the margins of society. Too often they result from the good-heartedness and will-power of a few individuals, in activities that remain exceptional. They are a long way from making up for the gaps which are appearing.

When the annual level of work diminishes by 12 per cent in ten years, while the nation's wealth increases, everyone ought to be able to claim the right to leisure. But how can that happen when unemployment has grown fivefold and its duration has doubled?

For the service sector to be more than an excuse, its dynamism must be allied with that of competitiveness in production, and public action must stimulate both simultaneously.

A problem for society

In short, we cannot avoid the problem of finding an overall conception of life in society. The idea of changing society at one blow is a dangerous dream, but the change that goes on in actually existing society is a permanent fact. It is expressed today in upheavals which affect us all and are dramatic for some. We must think about this process of change, if we are not to suffer from it. We must consider in which direction and how it can be led, how we can really influence it.

Many people today are suffering from inactivity and lack of opportunity to get back into society. Many needs, both old and new, are not being met by current activities. Between the two lie the market, business and the state. And, to be blunt, with these data and these tools we no longer know how to or even, sometimes, what needs to be done – definitely an unacceptable situation.

The first political requirement, therefore, is to find an appropriate answer to these questions. We will no longer turn back to past schemes for growth; we have to find a new social model which corresponds to the productive development, the needs and the maturity of society. This is a question for the whole world which is crucial for Europe and, most specifically, for France.

Finding a new model for Europe

Reality, being complex and diverse, does not allow itself to be reduced to a model. Yet that idea is convenient if we mean by it a stereotype which embodies major structural features, an operational logic which exists only as a tendency and around which one can observe many variations. With that reservation, we can think about the future of the social model for Euope.

Why, particularly, the model *for Europe*? Because twenty years ago, and perhaps even ten years ago, Europe seemed to be the place where one could perceive most completely the forms assumed by Keynesian regulation and the social conquests of industrial trade unionism. From vigorous social conflict to contractual power, diversity prevailed in a comparable structure of compromises, agents and regulations. There was the Fordist compromise in the work sphere, the role of wage scales, the centrality of the wages issue for social protection as a whole, and financial centralization of the insurance systems created by solidarity. In short, what we had was Fordist growth, regulated within national limits, with variable equilibria between regulation by institutions and by the market, the state and business, capital and labour. Most often, the trade unions and other organized elements played an essential intermediary role, with contractual negotiation and bipartite or tripartite management constituting the main forms of regulation.

Why this reference to Europe, when we are talking about *France*? Because France differs in several ways from this typical scheme.

The social and political upsurges of 1936, 1945 and 1968 undoubtedly resulted in major social conquests, but the feeble negotiating capacity possessed by the French labour movement can be clearly seen today as constituting a weakness. The social-democratic model, previously little esteemed by the French Left, is today a reference point deserving our attention, when we look at the

116

employment situation in Sweden or the bargaining power of the German trade unions.

Why, finally, this crucial emphasis on Europe? Because Europe is trying to find an identity amid the new facts of economic competition, and we know that the fate of Europe's inhabitants is interconnected. This is as true of France as of the other countries. If the Japanese model and Reaganite liberalism enjoyed such a vogue, that was due not merely to a wave of propaganda or a certain power struggle but also, to some extent, to our disarray in the face of our own difficulties. It was due also to some responsive elements which, though only partial, can account for the relative successes achieved by Japan and the United States, countries which found the springs of a new dynamism in their respective historical development. Their solution – partial and partly unsustainable – to the social problems inherent in economic changes was based upon the specific features of their societies. It is certain that Europe (and France in particular) must also seek its resources in its own history, if it is to develop in today's world.

An essential feature of Europe's industrial history is the place occupied by trade unionism and complementary forms of inter-mediation in the regulating of relations between individuals and groups and between groups and society. We must undoubtedly make use of that fact. In Sweden, for instance, occupational negotiation of industrial redeployment and training for new jobs has been, on the whole, successful. And, more or less everywhere in Europe, negotiations towards the modernization of business is going ahead more strongly than ever.

Making use of this resource presumes, however, that it is available. Yet trade unionism, especially in France, is not flourish-ing. The need to mobilize intelligence, to give incentives related to competence, and to call for active co-operation in order to ensure business success presents, as we have said, an opportunity for the world of labour. But we need a collective agent to give form to such a project. At present all we have is a few fragments of experience. The only active convergence of the European trade unions relates to the introduction of new technology. The only substantial advance in recent years is that achieved by the German metalworkers, who are advancing towards their midterm objective of a thirty-five-hour week by exchanging this reduction in working hours for the flexibility of a new way of producing.

We therefore need, while not renouncing the renewal of trade unionism, to seek elsewhere as well for the springs of a new coherence. The voluntary sector's dynamism in the creation of new services is far from negligible, but this development has to be financed. The repositioning of enterprises in competition has largely begun, but it is uneven and finds expression, on the whole, in a shrinkage of the production apparatus. Under these conditions, creating compensatory jobs is not enough to absorb the unemployed. Social protection, conceived as insurance against traditional risks, covers these risks only with difficulty when they worsen and diversify and is, moreover, incapable of preventing them. These are the three elements that have to be brought together, and this cannot be done without public action. But this action will not be enough by itself, nor should it come from the heights of state privilege. The partnership between public and private organisms is at one and the same time a new form of mixed economy and a new relationship between state and society. The state or the collectivity is the agent, but only along with others, and as prime mover rather than authority. This form of action overcomes the limits of public financing through the lever effect it exerts by mobilizing other resources and combining with them. It is highly suitable for decentralized activities based on initiative but co-ordinated on the appropriate scale of economies/territories. It also leaves room for conducting various experiments, relevant to different situations, from which the features of a new coherence will gradually emerge.

A new opportunity for France and for Europe

We are already seeing in many parts of Europe – in France as elsewhere – a certain number of experiments which bring together these two problematic elements – the new role of the trade unions in productive redeployment and the mixed territorial partnership for development.

The historical conjuncture of the changes under way can mean an opportunity for France in her distinctive situation and a chance for the countries of Europe to draw closer together. By mingling public action and the dynamism of organized society it affords an opportunity for progressive evolution in the French tradition of the centralizing state. The decentralization set in motion by the Left can constitute the path for this evolution, since the forms of public intervention, especially at regional level, have not yet been stabilized. We observe, moreover, a growth of partnerships for development. But if this dynamic is to prevail it will be necessary to combat the increasing frequency of party-orientated practices in the allocation of public funds, and other forms of electoral clientism. The choice lies between fertilization of economic or social initiative and a Balkanization of 'republics of grandees'.

In this still vague context the trade unions are taking more and more interest in important actions to bring about territorial development, and sometimes even taking part in them. Synthesis of these experiments with those of modernization negotiated within enterprises can constitute a basis for recomposition of a trade-union plan at the very moment when the national organizations are undergoing a serious identity and membership crisis. It is often when collapse threatens that one can at least set about rebuilding a house. The fact that the political bases of the split in the French trade unions are now changing very fast is also an opportunity to be grasped – but we must want to grasp it.

In choosing such a path, France would be drawing closer to the rest of Europe, where the social-democratic tradition and forms of organization are also being re-examined. The new experiments there are similar. The proximity of 1992 encourages such a *rapprochement*. This is not, in itself, a guarantee that it will be easy, but convergence of these experiments can be expedited by a harmonization of national systems of collective guarantees and social protection.

Understanding what is at stake

The preceding analysis and conclusions are meant to be pragmatic, and they deal above all with the relationship between competitive modernization and dynamism in society. This is indeed the essential framework for resolving the apparent dilemma between competitiveness and solidarity. However, it is not enough to make the creative forces which are at present constrained more dynamic or efficient. One must also quantitatively regulate incomes, social protection and employment, in an effective, solidary and acceptable way. All the forces in politics are looking for concrete remedies which may prove ineffectual or dangerous if one fails to grasp what is at stake in today's world.

Two principal ideas stand out in our analysis: the rise in interdependence, and the questioning of the state's role. They deserve some thought.

We have emphasized the fact that the growing interdependences in the world economy transform the conditions governing competition and justify the necessity of a European grouping.

At the other end of the human scale, the microeconomic performance of business depends on better interaction between the tasks and activities which contribute to production. The emergence, through the voluntary sector, of services which respond to a new demand is also an indicator of stronger interdependence on the microsocial scale, and a new relationship between individuals and the groups to which they belong. The thrust of local development brings these two basic trends together.

There is indeed a link between the globalization of production and the tightening of the relationship between immediate sociality and economic effectiveness: this is still the dialectic of social co-operation and the market. The question of the socialization of production, as Marx put it, reappears at a different level from that of the 1930s, giving rise to practical solidarities on the enterprise and regional scale, not in order to escape from the market but in order to face up to its requirements and to re-equilibrate competition through co-operation. Seen from this angle, socialization cannot be confused with a collectivism which would repudiate the individual. On the contrary, it implies that heterogeneous individuals and groups must necessarily get together.

To sum up this observation on contemporary capitalism, we can say that production is intimately social in nature, but that the system of ownership of its means causes it to be dominated by private-property tendencies. For more than a century economic crises and the forms of regulation which have enabled us to overcome them have revolved around this problem. Public policies tend as a rule to socialize whatever escapes the private logic of competition. This is true of macroeconomic action, industrial development, the training of the workforce, and the management of employment and social protection. Forms and mechanisms have varied, but since the beginning of this century – and especially since the crisis of the 1930s, and then the Second World War – conscious and organized socialization has been implemented within national frameworks and under the aegis of the respective states. What history shows us more strongly today is that one cannot confuse public management and socialization, state and society. To sum up: socialization takes hold of us simultaneously from above (on the global scale, which transcends that of the state) and from below (on the scale of daily life and work, which calls into question its relationship to society).

We undoubtedly need to invent conscious forms of socialization appropriate to these new conditions. Territorial partnerships are one such form: on the scale of an economy/territory they socialize the economic relations which stimulate development on a scientific and technological basis. This is a limited socialization, since it confronts the world market in which competition is intensified. The nurturing of new enterprises aims merely at making them stronger competitors, but it is also concerned with development and employment. In the United States they even talk about 'state development'. This idea is neither Democratic nor Republican – it is quite simply effective in the interests of the community.

Reason and experience may be applied to other social forms. For example, the social economy has been developed to only a limited extent in France. Why not try to make up for that in an all-European arena? This in turn could increase its potential within the national arena.

Managing the transitions

All these general ideas must be examined more practically in order to conceive a realistic transition to more adequate forms of solidarity. In the short term we have, first of all, to manage and improve what exists, but we must set in motion processes which can eventually transform it.

We have been shaped by more than one century. The nineteenth and twentieth centuries saw the rise of nationalities and the generalization of nation-states, together with the upsurge of industry. Production, trade and capital have long overstepped frontiers. Hitherto, however, people have talked of internationalization. Growth and the postwar alliances, the awakening of the Third World and the oil shocks, resulted in technological competition. We speak now of globalization, meaning the creation of a single economic space. This does not mean, though, that states, still less nations, have ceased to exist. What it does mean is that their particular logics will eventually have to be incorporated into wider regulations.

The real difficulty for Europe in this context is that its unity has not been constituted in the period now ending. On the contrary, it has been – even during the building of the Community – a crucible in which national interests have confronted each other. Important effects on the world market and intra-European political history come together to make even more crucial the questioning of national regulations and the role played in them by states.

Parallel to this, the global and normative form, the passive character of the mechanisms of redistribution no longer corresponds to economic conditions and the complexity of society. Increasing segmentation ruins social cohesion, the sense of solidarity and, in the end, competitiveness itself.

The so-called liberal answer will no longer do. It favours the richer and more successful at the expense of exclusion and misery for others. Moreover, its actual policies are very remote from its discourse.

What is in question is not the need for the state or major social institutions, but their forms and the way in which they are used. This question confronts everyone, whatever his or her purposes may be. It is the content of action that differs according to political orientations. For the Right, the state serves to fill in the cracks of a society which is unjust on the pretext of being efficient. For the Left, the state must be at the service of a plan for society. This difference has not changed, nor have the values which determine it. On the other hand, it is certain that the means must change progressively, the relationship to society no less than the scale of regulations. The constitution of an all-European social space, regionalization and decentralization are necessary components of this process. The financing and management of solidarity must be more directly linked with active social practices. Forms of aid and social activity must become more vibrant and must enter as much as possible into economic life.

However, these changes will not be brought about by a miracle, and they need time. It is therefore necessary also to maintain, while at the same time improving, the present functioning of national forms of solidarity. These must be made more flexible and compelled to converge in the European space, but not destroyed. And this is the whole argument. The cost of doing this is much easier to contemplate than the consequences of retreat. The permanent pretext of the rate of 'obligatory dues' is debatable. There is no sense in adding together VAT, income tax on individuals and companies, and social contributions linked to wages. The problems connected with the cost of labour and the state budget are difficult enough in themselves, without engaging in fictitious argument.

Maintaining the existing level of social protection is a condition for success in reforming it. In France, as in Europe, the transition to new forms will be complex and delicate. Since it is necessary, and even inevitable, this task must be undertaken and conducted without delay.

Reconstructing employment

Managing the transition presupposes, therefore, the permanence of the forms of solidarity that already exist, so long as the new ones have not taken over equally effectively. Herein lies – essentially in redistributive form – the social and political continuity of the process leading towards the future that must be built. But we also need a driving force capable of drawing all social mechanisms into a transformative process of change.

Much is said nowadays about a guaranteed minimum wage. Some see in this the instrument of a new social utopia; and others the inevitable price to be paid for a forced acceptance of the level of unemployment. Neither of these views can satisfy us: no overall dynamic could result from either. We fully support, as will be seen, a formula which ensures a survival minimum for all, whatever happens. But it would be just as absurd to make a panacea of this stopgap solution as to choose it as a way of solving the major problem of exclusion.

The most serious issue today, for most people, is not, primarily, income but employment. The damage done in *that* domain affects and can destroy the entire social structure of qualifications and jobs that exists at present. It is therefore here that the problem has to be tackled. The driving force of transition towards a new development must be the reconstruction of employment and its relations with different useful forms of activity.

Traditionally, employment policies have tended to favour the perpetuity of jobs and to organize movements aimed at securing full employment. Nobody nowadays dares to talk of such an objective. To be sure, we have understood that in this era better management of the marrying of supply and demand is not enough. But we are only just beginning to foresee the way things will develop and trying to organize training, initiations and reintegration into working life accordingly. It is absolutely necessary to go further – that is, to understand how new jobs are produced, and can go on being produced, in relation to other activities. In this connection – which is as much social as economic – we can define the place and the role of every instrument of an active employment and solidarity policy. Viewed in this way, the principal object of a policy is no longer to 'manage' the existing resources but to subordinate the form of this management to the content of the employment one is trying to reconstruct. This content must be the bearer of a development in employment. It must therefore base itself on the trends already in existence (but which, however, must be restructured) in business and in society. From this approach, a future view of active solidarity within a competitive setting can gradually follow.

FIFTEEN

Reconstructing Employment

CONTROVERSIES and policies in the sphere of employment are coming more and more to resemble the gold rush epic as seen in films. How many veins of ore have been imagined since 1973, and how many hopes disappointed? We will quote, without claiming to be exhaustive, some of the solutions put forward which, while not in themselves negative, were too simple and badly applied, and quickly revealed their limitations. There was the hope placed in the macroeconomic whole, either Keynesian or liberal. The reduction in the length of the working week did not prove convincing, either, at least in the way it was put into practice. The measures adopted for the social treatment of unemployment soon revealed their limitations in time, and their cost . . .

For want of ability to restore full employment, we are asked to forget about it. As some regret, unemployment appears to be 'an endemic disease, an unprecedented ailment which can, by homeostasis, take over an entire society'.[1] Unemployment, the acid rain of our society, attacks the social forest, causing it to lose density and vigour, beneath the helpless gaze of experts who explain its progress, forecasting this without being able to halt it.

Our approach is quite different. Starting from the observation of a gap between the immediate victory over unemployment and the long-term potential opened up by socioeconomic change and the emergence of new demands, we shall try to detach ourselves from short-term exigency and introduce the political necessities of employment in a medium-term procedure wherein planning and negotiation will again demonstrate their usefulness. The aim, then, is to identify the zones of breakdown and reconstitution.

A NEW MODEL OF EMPLOYMENT

The concepts which enable us to think about full employment in our industrial societies are not hard and fast. Categories like employment, organization of work, solidarity, and so on emerged at the end of the ninteenth century, established themselves between the world wars and underwent development during the 'thirty glorious years' of the postwar boom. Economists learn from social archaeology, and their attentive gaze into history's rear mirror enables them to grasp more successfully the changes that are now under way. Thus, 'the invention of unemployment'[2] was concomitant with the advance of the Industrial Revolution and compatible with standardized and Taylorized mass-production methods. In the face of economic and social hazards, the state became the indispensable, remote and anonymous mediator in industrial relations.

It is the maturation of the so-called Fordist forms of regulation that accounts for the duration and depth of the crisis. If we are to break with this movement, a 'Copernican revolution' will need to be begun and well thought out, with employment as a component. Let us, then, stop trying to bring back full employment in the form in which it existed. Let us locate the breaks that are beginning to appear in ways of using and managing the workforce, in order to determine ways of redefining and repairing them.

Chronicle of a death foretold

The laboratories of Utopia are not the only places where research is going on for alternatives to the productive system or opportunities for a different way of living and working. New economic and social practices and relations are being invented in business, in both workshops and offices.

The stimulus to this development comes from the modernization process initiated and required by technological change. What is new is the role accorded to technological innovation, which is no longer seen as an exogenous variable which entails a mere redistribution of abilities and functions. Business is undergoing a quiet revolution; options and strategies are undergoing profound changes. The most successful enterprises are those that think coherently about 'technological change, the content of work and the change in internal social relations', to quote Antoine Riboud's prophetic and very fruitful report *Modernization, A User's Manual*. According to this managerial approach, if employment is not thought about in a new way it will not be possible to use new technology profitably: 'Anyone who believes that cuts in numbers employed and investments in productivity will automatically increase profits fails to see that, nowadays, investments are ruinous if one does not take a completely new look at labour.'

Coming from the chairman of BSN, these statements do not lack credibility. What is at issue is the making of profound changes in the processes of integration – but also exclusion – of the workforce such as might draw the still vague outlines of a different kind of full employment.

A new logic of the integration of human resources is thus in operation. Technological innovation, product innovation and economies of scale – all furthered, with 1993 on the horizon, by a more open and more fluid internal European market – are some of the changes socialized by the professional and organization spheres. They find expression in forms of organization, management and remuneration which break with Taylorism – 'turning it upside down', as F. Dalle has said.

Towards the future paradigm

A new model of employment emerges from the break with the past. It is grounded, first and foremost, in a greater degree of worker autonomy, responsibility, motivation and involvement, valorized by a more individualized management of careers and wages. Moreover, the management of human resources is doubly integrated.

Integration of the tools of management with a view to constituting a sphere of qualification in which the dynamic of flows (hiring and firing) and transformations (internal mobility, training) of the workforce makes possible a forward-looking, dynamic and balanced management of employment. The human resources are interdependent with the other strategic variables, through aligning the management of employment with changes in investment and the requirements of commercial and financial policy.

Training plays an essential role in this schema, for it stimulates and accompanies the movement needed for change to take place: development of technical capacities and outlooks, access to cultures of participation and innovation, quality control in the face of fluctuations and risks. This point is important, because by enriching qualifications (polyvalence or polyaptitude) and ensuring a greater degree of continuity in periods of activity (work, maintenance, training) one reduces delays and the costs involved in responding to them. *Nil* defects, *nil* breakdowns, *nil* delays are challenges that can be met by this model of employment.

From the invisible hand to the invisible handshake

The convergence within a business of innovations in technology, products and social relations transforms the modes of production of work and employment by integrating them. Less than ever can the wage relation be reduced to a mere exchange, subject to the invisible hand of the market. Labour, a factor of production, is nevertheless not a mere commodity. Its efficacity is a condition of the profitability of technological innovation, and the management of human resources tends increasingly to become an investment.

The work contract has always been based on an uncertainty in the exchange it governs, since what it does is to make available a potential activity whose productivity and efficiency are not guaranteed. In the past this uncertainty has been partly reduced by means of factory discipline and rigid work organization. The death throes of Taylorism and the valorization of capacities for autonomy and mobilization dictate the use of new tools for labour and employment management.

Implicit contracts, formal investments – there is no lack of concepts for breaking with 'the invisible hand' by offering instead 'the invisible handshake'.[3] The enterprise ensures the quality and efficiency of the labour provided by guaranteeing its workers a certain autonomy, in terms of numbers employed and wage levels, in the face of economic uncertainty. This, of course, is not a new phenomenon, but it is beginning to become vital in the implementation of modernization in enterprises which systematize and individualize it (another novelty).

The flexibility debate must be considered differently. In the industrialized countries the introduction of adjustments to the numbers employed, and to wages, has brought about a lack of regulation in society. This has not led to the creation of jobs, owing to the resulting rigidities (a phenomenon of hysteresis) from large-scale and long-lasting unemployment. Above all, however, the forms of flexibility adopted are in contradiction to the new policies of business which treat their workforces as their 'most precious capital'.

How are training policies to be promoted unless the workforce concerned is stable? What worker can feel motivated and involved if he is not guaranteed a minimum of continuity in the work contract which binds him to his employer?[4]

It is a well-known fact that prolonged unemployment causes a qualitative deterioration in human capital: unsuitable qualifications, loss of motivation and a weakened capacity for reintegration. In consequence, a proportion of the unemployed drop out of the regulation and competition that goes on in the labour market. Wages and level of employment are then adjusted in line with the most recent arrivals, those who are more demanding and better qualified and will be the first to leave the queue. The dichotomy between workers who are integrated in the core and those on the periphery intensifies the difficulty of adjusting the labour market. The pressure of unemployment will be less strong on the sheltered workers, and their wages will be relatively independent of circumstances.

An essential lever for business adaptability is the valorization of human resources. Workers who are more competent and better motivated, and with whom one can discuss necessary flexibility measures – here we have a different conception. This flexibility is practised successfully by a growing number of enterprises. Competent workers are workers who are constantly in training to cope with technical change. When technical changes prove necessary, these workers are ready to take them on board, because they have been prepared. Workers become motivated when one appeals to their initiative, when their tasks are made as interesting as possible, and when they receive a clearly defined share of the results achieved by their efforts at productivity and their willingness to adapt. But motivation remains limited if the workers, or their representatives, are not treated as partners whom one informs and consults, and with whom one negotiates. This positive conception of flexibility gives priority to training, to professional mobility, to rearrangement of work periods, to a participatory system of management dealing with quality, productivity and the introduction of new technology, to a system of bonuses and/or clear, negotiated profit-sharing. It will aim at restricting recourse to precarious contracts and dismissals. Should the latter become necessary, good preventive management will take steps to prepare for them, to help them along and so to restrict their scale and the serious social consequences they can have for both the workers themselves and the local economic fabric.

In becoming richer, the sphere of workforce management expands. The enterprise, centred on its particular occupation, its main know-how, is initiated into new inter-enterprise relations, with a more externalized workforce now based equally on principles of specialization and of capacity. The quality of the products and services provided depends very heavily on the capacities of those workers situated on the periphery of the enterprise. A new sort of interdependence appears which, as R. Salais has pertinently observed, can open the way to institutional innovations, offering new contractual guarantees: 'an institutional system in which the management of economic uncertainty, and also of mobility and regrading, would be the responsibility of the group of enterprises in which the workers are active.'[5] Antoine Riboud responds positively by outlining the problem of the enterprise's civic responsibility: 'It must manage the way workers leave by putting as much effort into preparation and training as it puts into recruitment, and in its catchment area of employment it bears both an economic and a human responsibility.'

Such arrangements already exist. Town-planning regulations, conversion contracts, the industrial groups' 'DATA' [the *Délégation à l'Aménagement du Territoire et à l'Action Régionale* is a body charged with combating excessive centralization], rules governing the quality of subcontracted work, transfers of personnel from one establishment to another. . . . Their systematization through negotiation, in a decentralized way, would favour new forms of workforce regulation which, while not abolishing dualism, would mitigate its effects. A new dynamic of employment would then be based, within the framework of expanded spheres of workforce management, on the arranging of transitions, the organizing of routes for change.

A co-operative system of management can emerge, relying on an economic and social network that makes possible compensatory strategies in favour of employment, limiting the effects of confinement in low-skilled, insecure jobs, and promoting preventive management.

SOLIDARITY RENEWED

So businesses, especially the larger ones, are taking the first steps towards new negotiated and decentralized ways of regulating their workforce, based on diversified systems of direction and based redeployment. The frontiers between the internal and external labour markets are becoming blurred, and the gap between the core and the peripheral workforce is narrowing.

This new model does not provide an answer to all the imbalances of employment and, in particular, to the crucial question of drifting in the labour market, of paths that lead to exclusion and poverty. One must take special care not to depict the future which is coming into being in the style of a wish-fulfilment novelette. The coin of this model of a more advanced integration of human resources has a reverse side, with additional risks and modes of exclusion.

A recurring spiral of exclusion

Economic problems, with a high and rising level of unemployment which is lasting longer, have caused new forms of exclusion to appear. Hitherto sheltered strata of the population have been suddenly plunged into insecurity, instability and almost total lack of income. This external and 'absolute' poverty differs from the traditional kind, which had not been ameliorated by growth and social policies and resulted from a series of disadvantages. The new forms of exclusion are not subject to this logic of plurality and reduplication of disadvantage; they are caused by see-saw mechanisms in situations which deteriorate rather rapidly. Insecurity is central to the process of exclusion – insecurity of income, combined with irregularity in its amount and availability. Uncertainty about resources, indeed, coupled with an unreliable job situation and the resultant repeated unemployment. One thing that can halt the sequences of events that lead to poverty is a heritage, in the broadest sense – financial, but also human. A training, a qualification and a stable family increase a person's capacities for resistance and facilitate reintegration into work.

The system of social protection created in a period of economic expansion, weighted down as it is with successive layers of sediment and subject to serious financial constraints, cannot cope adequately with these new phenomena. Holes therefore appear in the safety-net of social protection. An inquiry carried out by the CNAF [*Conseil National des Associations Françaises*] estimates that 5 per cent of families (about 200,000) with at least one child have resources of less than fifty francs per day per person. On its part, INSEE has identified 'a very strong presumption' of poverty in 400,000 households (headed by someone under sixty) which receive neither income from work nor unemployment pay. The complexity and multiplicity of its causes make this phenomenon hard to deal with. There is a concatenation of difficulties, but lack of a job is the essential element in exclusion processes. Reconstructing employment is the principal way to break open the trap which closes on an increasing number of workers in insecure jobs. The proliferation of transitional situations and insecure jobs reduces the prospects for stable integration. This does not necessarily lead to poverty, but it does increase the risk.

It is the process of workforce allocation linked with present-day conditions of modernization that destabilizes individuals who are in a weak position and puts exclusion at the very heart of the way the socioeconomic system functions. Without corrective structural action, it seems inevitable that this phenomenon will spread.

The employment system, as we have seen, is like a comet whose nucleus shrinks while its halo expands. That is nothing new. In the 1960s the segmentation of the labour market was already a well-known fact. The distinctive features of the present situation are etched in the new models of human resources management, which exacerbate the risks of rejection and change its nature. The flow of steady skilled jobs is less plentiful than it used to be, because new technologies are less rich in job opportunities, and skill requirements are changing.

Technological and organizational changes are associated with new figures in the world human labour. In place of the image of the 'well-off wage-earner' we find new professional and social identities. For businesses, the success of technological change and modernization depends fundamentally on human behaviour. This is the reason for the fastidious attention given to internal workforce evaluation and recruitment criteria. As the Lesourne Report noted, the compensating feature of the development of organizational

methods is that businesses seek individuals who can accept responsibility, can work either in groups or independently, and are
adaptable. There will also be a rise in the level of qualifications
demanded.

Lack of competence, insufficient paper qualifications, failure to
conform to the mould of the new professional identity will
destabilize workers who have jobs and block their access to stable
employment. These new social divisions intensify the threat of
marginalization and the prospect of pauperization.

Reconstructing employment means looking for solutions to
these situations of exclusion, both old and new, which affect
economic, social and political cohesion. Families and individuals
who face the future with anguish are becoming ever more
numerous. Enough to eat, somewhere to live, keeping one's
children at home, looking after oneself – this is the daily horizon of
these poor people. Such intolerable dependence is the common
denominator for all the excluded. These citizens' absolute poverty
deprives them of economic, social and cultural rights, and prevents
them from really enjoying their civil and political liberties.

This social failure of democracy is much more serious than the
economic mess that accompanies it. Overcoming it is the essential
challenge that we must take up. Contemporary history shows that,
even more than a moral requirement, this is a political necessity.

Bringing employment policies and social protection policies together

Response to the challenges of exclusion thus seems to be both a
social and economic necessity and the precondition for a living and
stable democracy. Without exaggerating the risks, and aware that
history never repeats itself exactly, we must nevertheless see that
this is a major issue in social and economic policy. Donzelot has
written that the 'social' dimension appeared on the morrow of the
Industrial Revolution as an invention that was needed if a society
choosing democracy was to be governable. Today, renewal of
solidarity seems to be as the precondition for strengthening

democracy. It should contribute to the decline of 'political passions'. This way of looking at the 'social' factor may be seen in the renewal of political thought in the United States on the subject of justice in relation to law. John Rawls[6] is the originator of a theory of justice as equity. He defines the basic structure of a modern constitutional democracy, a unified system of social co-operation, in accordance with two fundamental principles: liberty and difference. According to the latter principle, the degree of justice in a society may be assessed in relation to the fate in store for its most deprived members. This is how he justifies unequal measures to the benefit of the most disadvantaged.

The mechanisms that operate in the development of absolute poverty result from progressive slippages in which insecurity of employment and resources is combined with individual weaknesses. This dynamic perception of a process of exclusion leads one to favour changing and differentiated exclusion-reduction policies which combine restoration of minimal economic and social rights (income, housing, health) with active strategies of social and professional reintegration. Employment policies and social protection policies must combine to build a lasting strategy for the fight against poverty.

The first aspect of this strategy must be preventive. Where education is concerned there must be, according to the Bertrand Schwartz Report, positive discrimination in employment. An early and differentiated treatment of situations of unemployment can limit the processes of exclusion linked with long-term unemployment. To avoid having to resort to burdensome support measures after long periods of unemployment, priority must be given to attacking, without delay, the disadvantages suffered by those who have recently fallen into unemployment.

We can then distinguish certain guiding principles to be applied to the drift into unemployment. In the first two or three months of their registration, unemployed people receive a limited payment from the job centre. From the third month onwards a more thorough examination and follow-up must check, first and foremost, on the guaranteed resources at the disposal of the individuals concerned, and their families. Furthermore, one must single out those who could find a job if they were given just a little help, as against those who suffer from more serious disadvantages in trying to get back into the labour market. All available means must then be mobilized – information, placement, advice, training. After the sixth month of unemployment, personal interviews and evaluations are necessary. At this stage – following the Danish model of combating unemployment – one should give each unemployed person a right to reintegration. Before the ninth month of unemployment they should be offered either a job, in the public or the private sector, or training leading to a qualification, or socially useful activity, remunerated on a scale closely tied to the SMIC [*Salaire Minimum Interprofessionel de Croissance* – guaranteed minimum wage]. Specific funding for business, local communities and the various voluntary organizations should accompany this right.

The second aspect entails ensuring a minimum reintegration income, because however effective preventive measures and tightening up social protection measures may be, there will still be holes in the net. Creating this minimum income calls for supplementary steps. In particular, one must make sure of certain implementational principles which ensure its efficacy and, in a way, its durability. Jean-Michel Belorgey lays down some useful guidelines in this area in his book *La Gauche et les pauvres*.

This arrangement must be national in its scope and complement the basic social protection system, so that its beneficiaries are not marginalized further. It is based on a guaranteed resource proportional to family size, the amount to be decided as a percentage of the SMIC. It is therefore paid as an addition to other resources, without any time limit but with a periodic re-examination of beneficiaries' situations. It must also be accompanied by opportunities for training and reintegration. In particular, access to socially useful jobs or to training should be encouraged. Finally, and with the same will to promote reintegration, the fight against poverty must be reconciled with the maintenance of encouragement to work. In particular, acceptance of part-time or temporary work ought not to prevent someone from receiving the full amount or part of the minimum income.

TIME REGAINED

Organizing and managing time, whether it is work time, time spent in voluntary unpaid activity or free time, constitutes one of the central problems of our society, poised as it is between demands for individual autonomy and expansion and the need for collective management of employment. It is not possible to contemplate an overall economic development that would combine rapid increase in productivity, gains, persistence of a rather slow rate of growth and, above all, reduction in underemployment, without accepting at the same time that the average length of working time is going to diminish.

Yet it has been too quickly concluded that the reduction of working hours could be abandoned as an effective instrument of employment policy. France, it was thought, would get lazy, becoming an island of idleness and slackness in a world wherein efficiency and output require everyone to work more, not less. Our chief competitors were pointed to as examples, and incomplete international comparisons were offered. . . . These were bitterly refuted. The model country, the Federal Republic of Germany, is showing signs of 'weakening'. In the West German steel industry, following the example set by the metal industry, employers and trade unions arrived at an agreement reducing the working week to thirty-six-and-a-half hours – not with a cut in wages but, on the contrary, with an increase: of 2 per cent in 1988 and a further 2 per cent the following year. Similarly, in the public services the working week is to be reduced, in two stages, to thirty-eight hours. This has not happened without conflict (remember the metalworkers' strike in 1984) or controversy. The socialist O. Lafontaine caused a stir by proposing that full wage compensation should be abandoned in the case of the highest-paid. Nevertheless, reduction in the length of the working week has ceased to be a taboo subject and is seen as a measure that could contribute to improving the employment situation.

In France hitherto our social organization, our negotiation procedures, our culture, and the heterogeneity of demands and situations have prevented us from making significant progress in this domain. That is not a reason for giving up the task. Let us remember that more than five million wage-earners are still working forty or more hours per week.[8]

On Method

We must gravitate from a defensive, uniform, Malthusian conception of work time reduction to an aggressive, varied and fruitful conception of the contractual organization of elective time.

The idea of a mechanical division of jobs by a sort of rule of three does not work. On the one hand, jobs are more and more personalized, and extensive personnel substitutions are difficult to carry out. On the other, only a minority of workers are willing to accept a reduction in pay in exchange for more free time. Most of them neither want nor are able to accept that, and then there is the question of production costs. The contribution made to improving the quality of life by an overall reduction in working hours is only slight. Those days when reduction in working hours essentially served the purpose of protecting workers against excessive working hours are no longer with us. The addition of a few minutes of free time each day, or a few days' more holiday each year, no longer alters people's lives in the way that elective time can alter them.

However, this is not a reason for leaving the question of arranging reductions in working hours on the back burner. While a policy in which everyone marches in step seems inappropriate, concrete solutions may be found in specific cases. Arrangements aimed at reducing working hours and experiments, either individual or collective, in elective time are, provided they are properly controlled, an important instrument for increasing productivity, creating jobs or limiting dismissals. Henceforth they will form part of the modernization process, as was well shown by the Taddei Report (1985), and sometimes, faced with the threat of unemployment, real and practical solidarity operations are organized at enterprise level. The ingenuity of the social partners is progressively exercised and refined. It would be a pity not to make more use of the tool thus forged.

Yet that is the risk being run at the moment by the social debate. From now on the question of working hours is in danger of being tackled only from the narrow angle of flexibility – and that, moreover, with a narrow, limited, typically 'provincial-French' outlook. Reduction in working hours would be one possible concession (but not the only one[9]) to be included in an updating process aimed at enabling a company to modulate working hours and exceed the legal maximum of thirty-five hours a week without paying overtime. It is clear that annualization of working hours is what is needed, but this should not be all a time policy means. Workers also have the right to their own forms of flexibility, variable timetables – elective time in various forms. In general, it is necessary to organize collectively and individually, wherever this can be done, the opportunity to choose between more income and more time.

Is it necessary to point out that what distinguishes part-time work from elective-time work is, first, that elective time may result in more work rather than less being done,[10] and, second, that this position is always reversible? The Workers must always be able to go back, whenever they so wish, to the collective timetable, subject to certain conditions of procedure and detail.[11] This means that elective time, usually individual (though one can imagine freely chosen formulas for multiple collective timetables), can be correctly organized only collectively and contractually, after a close examination of workplaces, conditions for replacement, and so on (in fact, conditions very similar to those which have to be created in order to bring off a collective operation to reduce the length of working hours). Elective-time work, unlike part-time work, does not mean insecurity, so long as reversibility is assured. It is a form of flexibility without insecurity, for the benefit of the worker and favouring the development of personal ways of life. So much the better if this greater control by everyone of their own time has the indirect consequences of facilitating a flexible division of labour.

We can therefore see that the angles of time policy are specific but converge towards common results, on condition that the multi-dimensional character of time organization is properly taken account of, and all the interests involved are acknowledged. Time policy must be global, multidimensional, decentralized . . . and coherent.

A careful relaunch of the various policies for arranging work-time reductions

Here we need to find the right tone. Work-time reductions are neither a poison fatal to competitiveness nor the magic potion for curing unemployment. They contribute to the modernization of business, to the fight against unemployment and to the development of personalities. They form one component among others in the magic marriage of competiveness and solidarity to which French society aspires. They aim not so much at 'sharing work' as one shares a cake (an odd sort of cake, incidentally) as at expanding employment dynamically to make it more accessible to those who have been deprived of it. Working less, perhaps, but in the end working more collectively, whether in paid or unpaid activity.

This means that the irreconcilable conflict between those who say we should work more (so as to be more competitive) and those who say we should work less (so as to share jobs) is sterile and false.

Work more? Yes, if it is a matter of strictly fulfilling renegotiated timetables. Yes, if it is a question of asking, at a given moment, people who possess some particular skill or creativity, for whom there is no substitute on the labour market, to increase their work effort, if only for a time.

No, if what is meant is lengthening workers' collective time-tables without increasing their pay. Is it not obvious that this might result in a reduction in the numbers employed, and that it means actually cutting hourly rates of pay? If this *has* to be done, let us say it must be done and do it, but with the same timetable. Then, at least, it will be possible to maintain or increase the numbers employed.

Work less? No, if this is sure to reduce business competitiveness.

Yes, if the opposite is true. There is indeed no disadvantage in people working less if what they do can be done by others, without extra cost to the enterprise.

Three vital conditions

The conditions which make successful arrangements for reducing working hours possible have now been defined clearly enough.

They must not entail extra cost, in any form, for the businesses concerned – which assumes that the productivity of the machinery is increased, or that the level of payment received by the workers is only partially maintained.

Businesses must be able to find on the labour market the workers needed to provide replacements.

Such operations as are undertaken must be negotiated and agreed between social partners, and the level on which these negotiations take place must be as close to the shop floor as possible. Not only is the national level less and less appropriate – except for providing a general framework – but this is also true of the branch of industry and sometimes even of the company. It is the level of the establishment, and sometimes of the workshop or the service, that is best for this purpose.

The public authorities ought not to compel anything to be done, nor ought they to do nothing: their task is to encourage action. Therefore, would not a reduction in dues or taxes help, first and foremost, those who act dynamically on time management and job-sharing? After all, that would constitute a fair return for the savings they make for the community in unemployment pay and in avoiding the social traumas caused by unemployment. One can imagine, for instance, a tax credit, a reduction in the rate of company tax, for companies which have shortened their hours. Similarly each taxpayer might be allowed to save, without paying tax on it, one year's income, this money to be used only to finance periods of inactivity, voluntary or not, partial or total, and only then, being taxed. Thanks to this 'savings-time', periods of elective free time (voluntary part-time work, family holidays, sabbaticals, etc.) could be budgeted for. This would create a financial product that would be much more dynamic on the social or employment level than the recently announced plan for savings for retirement. Finally, participation funds could, by special agreement between social partners, be used to finance operations for arranging reductions in working hours or formulas for elective time.

At a moment when re-establishment of business accounts and of global economic balances makes it possible to envisage, for the future, a little more flexibility in profit-sharing, it would be really reprehensible not to explore the possibilities, for workers, of a choice between an increase in purchasing power and a reduction in working time which would help employment.

SIXTEEN

Freeing Society

POLICY cannot be a mere reflection of a society, and still less of its passing moods or whims. This is why I have emphasized the restoration of the republican state. We have had enough of those incisive thoughts on total state withdrawal, as though it were a sort of monstrous machine plonked down on society with, as its intrinsic logic, 'living its own life' at the risk of stifling the inner dynamism of society.

How are we to find the essential synergy between an active state which animates and a free society? We have tried to give some first replies to that question, aimed at provoking discussion and stimulating analysis and thought. What is at stake is the moral health and material strength of our nation.

Living collectively according to common values

The natural movements that stir a society do not necessarily lead it towards a rational evolution. The common good does not emerge spontaneously; the measure of a policy's greatness is that it succeeds in bringing it to birth, but does so with the will and co-operation of all members of the given society.

In other words, the society's destiny does not depend exclusively on the logic of the market and its invisible hand. Yet is this not how all our liberals argue, along with everyone who counterposes, for example, competitiveness to solidarity? It is true that reconciling the two is a delicate matter; it implies an awareness that is hard to come by, whereas economic constraint is so strong and seems to impose on us the model of 'the fox in the henhouse'.

This is why we have striven, in this book, to show that economic performance depends not only on the general economic environment and the quality of leaders, but also on the contribution made by every member of business or the community.

Besides, is not society effecting spontaneous breakthroughs in that direction? Just consider the resilience of the most efficient enterprises, the reasons behind the forward leap made by a particular territorial community, the innovations in the life of the voluntary sector. They show us the way ahead and, sometimes unwittingly, meet up with the essential values.

First of all, equality of opportunity. How much wealth is lost by an education system that has remained, like our society, so elitist! What talents remain unexploited owing to a work organization system that rejects any active participation, any new proposal! The French hierarchical system is tough. It resists, even while Taylorism is in retreat. It dominates in our administation. In order to overthrow this fortress, even though it has fortunately been undermined by experiments in participation and partnership, we must begin with the schools, by creating a climate of lifelong education and encouraging all talents to bloom. Is this not also the way to undermine the foundations of future exclusions? The person excluded is, above all, someone who no longer knows who they are or what they can do to get out of the vicious circle of marginality.

If a person who is in difficulties no longer knows how to escape from them, he or she applies to a 'guichet', to an administration. They want to exercise their rights – provided, first of all, that they know what they are. And that, as everyone will agree, is far from easy, given the complexity of our laws and rules. From particular cases to new problems, our state insurance system has become a waste of money. It is an instrument which, while very expensive, is less and less effective. Everyone has their overall solution to this problem: abolishing some rights and – in the sacred formula – making individuals responsible; reducing the rate of financial cover; creating new rights, such as the indispensable minimum income.

These reforms, some of which are adequate up to a point, will not fill the vacuum created by a society which shifts all responsibility for solidarity on to public institutions. It is not a question of bringing back the golden age of a mainly rural society in which many misfortunes were taken care of by the family or local milieu. Nor is it a question of dreaming of a perfect society in which inter-personal solidarity will reign supreme.

But it *is* necessary to put correctly the central problem of life in common: how are we to encourage those neighbourly solidarities which will give our society a different look from that of communities which have broken up or become indifferent? Minorities are at work on this task, setting examples. Who talks about them, who helps them? Policy's role is to conceive the structures that will favour the spread of these solidarities. But the question is also put radically to all the actors in civil society: trade unions, voluntary associations, new forms of business. A dual movement of the state and of society, as it were – one illustration among others of the necessary synergy.

In other words, we have to go over from the passive society to the active society. The seeds of this change are already germinating. What we must do is help them to flourish.

We are gradually drawing nearer to this idea of a different model of development, integrating these new solidarities but also responding to needs that the market fails to reveal: the fight against the devastation or neglect of nature, the planning of our towns and countryside, the opportunities offered by better use of free time, the social needs linked with the organization of work or with segregation by age group.

'All partners in development.' Examples abound to show what

can be achieved by a community which mobilizes all its members and all its talents. This can be a region, a catchment area for employment, a town, or a district within a town. Let us not be too pessimistic. Let us not neglect the experiments which have proved successful. But let us give them a minimum of political formality and call upon the state to adapt its behaviour and its means of action to them.

Freeing the state

Everything has been said about the state, and from every angle. Yet it still remains to nationalize it and free it.

Nationalize it, by returning it to its citizens – not as a mere practical instrument but as the expression of a common good to which we aspire. Despite decentralization, a psychology of distance continues to separate government and governed. The latter still expects too much from the state, to the point that many *députés* admit that they have become social workers. It is fitting of course, that a *député* should help in preparing and submitting an application, in finding jobs, and in the creation of new activities in his constituency. He might even come to adopt our slogan: 'All partners in development'. But you can have too much of a good thing. The administration itself must feel that it is in society 'like a fish in water'. It too can, without violating its principles, become a partner in the development of society.

Freeing the state means ridding it of all those hidden feudalisms which influence and hinder it. These could be the corporations which are so well implanted in the ministries that the latter too often consider that the general interest coincides with the interests of these professional groups. Or the trouble may be the relations between public authority and big business groups – the most recent, and very eloquent, instance of which has been provided by the constitution of organized 'cells' within the privatized firms.

The rules of the game

Is France unalterable, living a life of cosy conservatism while allowing herself, from time to time, some outbursts of revolt to excite the chroniclers? One might think so if one were to recall 1953, 1963, 1968 or, most recently, 1986. These sudden movements immediately give rise to learned interpretations which are partly correct. And then life goes on again . . . just as before. There remain, to remind us that we are citizens, periodic elections . . . and the televised performances of our National Assembly on Wednesday afternoon – usually a very poor show, counter productive to democracy and citizenship.

Yet each stormy episode in our public life leaves traces that often go deep, especially May 1968, now underestimated, having formerly been overexalted. Everything happens as though we do not know how to reap the harvest sown by those who express revolt, disenchantment and frustration. Behind their demands, frequently, hides the desire for a different way of life, potentially a positive contribution to our society.

The poverty of our public life may thus be explained not merely by the decline (which is doubtless temporary) of ideology, or by the irruption of visual forms of communication. It cannot be linked exclusively with one particularly empty moment in our history. It is due also to the lack of synergy between the state and civil society, to the retreat of the mediations which are indispensable to democracy – parliamentary assemblies and trade unions, to mention only the most striking examples.

Where should we begin? A pointless question. Let everything be put back in its rightful place. For this to happen there is no need to undertake a fresh reform of our institutions. It is enough simply to return to the actual spirit of democracy and the duties of the republican state. The French people, if clearly invited to participate in the common good, will do the rest. And they are capable of doing it.

149

SEVENTEEN

Our Europe

T HE construction of a united Europe signifies, politically and
historically, an exceptional opportunity for France – the
France that exists today, with her assets and her weaknesses. (But
what country is without these?)

Some imply that the National Front successes are due in part to
a sort of forgetting of national sentiment in the argument and
struggle for Europe.

In the first place, this reasoning telescopes several complex
social data. Le Pen obviously gains from the breakdown and
exclusion processes associated with the modernizing and global-
izing of the economy. It is understandable that, in this context,
many social groups are turning towards what has always been the
locus of their defence and their conquests – namely, the national
community.

But the crucial point is that the national community can no
longer fulfil that function on its own. The consequence of globalization would be much more severe without the construction of
Europe. This is what we have to make clear, in a crucial battle of
ideas.

In the short term, the real problem is that it has been necessary, in order to get Europe moving again, to accelerate the unification of the market in advance of the construction of the shared space. This has resulted in upsets for various social groups, but the answer can only be an intensified effort to construct the social space and develop economic co-operation. This is the only way to bring under control the forces at work in the economy of Europe and the world. All those who propagate the idea of a direct link between Europe and the rise of the National Front would be better advised to reread the history of French politics, of the successive examples of movements based on rejection of necessary changes, defence of corporate interests and inevitably, racism. They might also, with an examination of their consciences which is rather overdue, ask themselves whether the spectacle they present to our fellow-citizens is likely to mobilize them in the service of an ideal, and of their country. The poverty of our political debates accounts, in no small measure, for the resurgence of extremism.

In a world which is as unforgiving as ever, still facing many threats, and in which peace, democracy and freedom are never definitively gained, it is important to raise the battle of ideas to a higher level and provide substance for noble collective ambitions. A united Europe is one of these, though certainly not the only one. We show in this book that there are other fields of work available to the younger generation in which they can become aware of their potential, exercise their responsibilites and, consequently, recover confidence in a shared, collective future.

In other words, Europe is not a panacea. It would be foolish to wait for Christmas 1992, in order then to hang up one's stocking by the chimney in the hope of finding in it, at the beginning of 1993, the wrapped present of a Europe miraculously unified, with a prosperous economy, declining unemployment, and uncontested authority in the world.

No, the battle has to be waged every day – as it has been, successfully, during the last four years – to build a political and economic entity commensurate with our ideals and our ambitions, an entity in which France will be even more France than she is today, because she is stronger economically and more influential intellectually and politically. And the same forecast could be made

152

for each of the twelve countries that make up the Community. What is essential, said Jean Monnet, is that 'there should be no more separate national actions, but European actions instead'. What is essential, one might add today, is to exercise our sovereignties together, rather than play a petty game based on the illusion that our national sovereignty can influence events by itself.

Thus, France will grow in stature by means of Europe, as Europe, a group of middle-ranking nations, asserts itself as a first-ranking power.

The economic leap forward

The fear of 'economic Europe' is, when all is said and done, only the latest form of an ambiguous inferiority complex. Why should we be incapable of using all the opportunities offered by the great market of three hundred and twenty million consumers? This prospect is the only one that enables us – or, as some see it, compels us – to adapt ourselves to the new world context, to remedy our threefold weakness, which is shared to a greater or lesser extent by our eleven partners: inadequate competitiveness, relative weakness of economic growth, an intolerable level of unemployment.

Whatever their size, their greater or lesser degree of specialization, their dependence on a world market or a local market, our businesses can perform on the three registers offered by the progressive realization of a common economic space: dimension, co-operation, cohesion.

The dimension effect offered by the great market, the objective of 1992, is the best known. Figures have been quoted on economies of scale and the positive fallout from the abolition of all trade restrictions, to which should be added the opportunities presented by a common strategy for growth based on closer co-operation between macro economic policies and monetary policies.

The companies who benefit will be those which succeed in anticipating the opportunities offered by the opening up on the markets or the harmonization of standards, for example. Investment and diversification strategies need to be re-examined on the pan-European scale, which will be the operational base for the global policy of large-scale enterprises.

To be competitive on one's own or jointly with others? This is undoubtedly the most urgent question that faces many of our business chiefs now that the building of Europe is well under way. How are they to strengthen specialization, establish the necessary links and partnerships, reach the critical threshold, defend themselves against 'raiders'? This is where the power of the second lever comes in: co-operation.

It is, indeed, in the dialectic between competition and co-operation that it will be possible to realize, not a mere free-trade area exposed to every passing wind, but a shared space of benefit to all. Hence the European research programmes, the best-known of which are ESPRIT, for electronics, and RACE, for telecommunication. Hence, too, some earlier achievements, such as Ariane and Airbus, which show that, under the twofold pressure of scientific progress and the globalization of the economy, facts have preceded political decisions. Hence the EUREKA programme, launched by François Mitterrand, which is to the imminent shared market activities what the community programmes are to the imminent pre-competitive research activities.

Is there any point in recalling that businesses of all sizes have participated in all these projects? Small and medium-sized enterprises, for example, have been notably successful within the ESPRIT framework. But that was not enough – which is why the European Commission has set up and expects to develop a network of Euro-info centres which provide more modest-sized companies not only with all the information they need but also with opportunities to come together and work jointly, regardless of distance and frontiers.

Economic growth still has to reach all regions, and all regions must be in a position to mobilize all their resources, both human and natural. There will be no success for Europe if we do not offer equal opportunities to all regions and, consequently, to all businesses and all workers. This is the third lever, that of cohesion, which is assumed by the implementation, on the European level, of common policies to bring aid to regions which have lagged behind in modernization, industrial regions in the throes of painful redeployment, and rural regions which are being doubly affected by migration to the towns and the forced-march modernization of agriculture. To indicate the orders of magnitude, we can estimate that these policies, as they have been planned, will contribute to an average 1 per cent increase in economic growth, and more for the backward regions.

French enterprises, in agriculture, industry and the service sector, are affected by these prospects. From now on they must include them in their policies, whether individual or sectoral. They could find no better springboard for ensuring their future – their outlets, their investments, and their general strategies.

Making a success of decentralization

This reform was put into effect in 1981, under the aegis of Gaston Defferre, with the full support of François Mitterrand, who has always regarded decentralization as the best antidote to traditional and encroaching statism. The regionalists used, among other arguments, that of distance from Paris. To this will be further added the argument of distance from the levels at which the European Community's decisions are taken.

A look ahead enables us, in fact, to define, for the future, three great centres of economic and social dynamism: the Community, the Nation (which will retain, in every way and for a long time to come, a key role), and the Region.

On the balance between these three centres of decision will depend the vitality of the European whole. What better illustration can one give than the trump cards held by Germany in the shape of its federal structure, its *Länder*? The *Land* is both a place where individuals and activities are rooted and a centre of initiative and dynamism capable of mobilizing and arranging the available resources. The *Länder* also reflect the full diversity of geographical, economic and social situations.

Far be it from us to want to impose that structure upon France. But let us underline one of the weaknesses of French-type

155

decentralization, from the point of view of effectiveness: too many powers for the *département* and not enough for the region.

The *département* has inherited, in accordance with our tradition, many powers, supported by substantial financial resources. However, it is too small to conceive and achieve the necessary economic and social development. The region is a good size for this purpose, but possesses only limited powers. In the interests of France in tomorrow's Europe, it is vital to reconsider the very foundations of our decentralization and to give the regions the means to realize their legitimate ambitions in the spheres of economic, social and financial activity.

To be convinced of this, one need only observe the enthusiasm and pugnacity with which France's southern regions took part in the pilot scheme, designated as such by the European Commission, of the Integrated Mediterranean Programmes – that is, those programmes which were originally designed to enable these regions to cope with the consequences of the enlargement of the Community to include Spain and Portugal. The French regions were the most ready to mobilize themselves and show enthusiasm. They put forward high-quality plans, having discovered, in the course of drawing them up, all the potential of a more self-sufficient mode of development.

Strengthening the power of the regions, as necessitated by the progress of Europe, will mean making a big contribution to the conception of this new development model. It will help to restore balance to our democratic life and diversify our political debate. It will bring us to the opposite situation to the one in which, alas, we are now living, where key people, when affected by the rules forbidding plural mandate, relinquish the chairmanship of their region so that they can retain both their mandate as *député* or *sénateur* and the chairmanship of the General Council of a *département*, because that is where the electorate can really see them in action.

If it is not adapted to the new realities of Europe and France, this great future reform, bogged down in our traditions and too deeply tainted by the past, is in danger of withering away.

Intellectual and political influence

As we see from this example, France is not taking the path that might ensure for her, in the Europe of tomorrow, the intellectual and political influence to which she should by right aspire.

So, then, the whingers will say, we French are to borrow deregulation from the Anglo-Saxons, monetary stability and federalism from the Germans, the modern spirit of enterprise from the North Italians. We are, indeed, often guilty of provincialism, and it is only with some reluctance that we admit, in our heart of hearts, that there is much to be learnt from the experience of our European partners.

More optimistic souls, though, could draw up an impressive list of the influences we have exerted, starting with the influence of those Frenchmen who, in the last forty years, have been at the forefront of the successful construction of Europe – not forgetting, since we are not only political thinkers and architects of policy, such exemplary industrial initiatives as Ariane or Airbus, the great successes (which have set a precedent) of our agriculture, and our contribution to the scientific progress accomplished in Europe.

Let us, therefore, beware, even while expecting a great deal of ourselves, of any sort of masochism which might lead to a strenthening of French provincialism and rejection of the 'open sea' that lies before us.

What is the principal difficulty? Undoubtedly it lies in our mistaken concentration, in our political debates, on our internal quarrels: conflicts between personal ambitions, intensified by the prospect of the presidential election; battles between political party workers over how the Right or the Centre is to be recomposed; indulgent harkings back to our great confrontations in the past . . .

Many French people would be amazed if they knew that in the European councils which bring together the heads of state and government of our twelve nations, a broad consensus emerges, on the problems of society or on the social dimensions of Europe's construction, between two of the major political currents in our Europe: the Socialists and the Christian Democrats.

As we have said, there is a European model of society to which the great majority of Europeans are committed. Everyone agrees that we must adapt it, in order to respond better to the dual challenge of economic competition and solidarity. Nevertheless, most people want to retain its spirit and its political foundations.

Let us not try to find, in recognition of this fact, some mental reservation regarding what in France is called the opening to Europe. No, what is more obvious here is an illustration of the solid foundations of our Europe, and a call to switch the political debate, unequivocally on to what unites us and gives us strength, and what differentiates us but also constitutes strength for us – a Europe united in diversity.

France definitely cannot stand aside either from this debate or from the movement that is taking us into the third millennium. With so many talented people among our politicians, with intellectuals and scientists eager to make their contribution to the common thought process, how could we miss this opportunity to be, at one and the same time, both useful to France and indispensable to Europe?

European progress in movement and clarity

'Nobody falls in love with a growth rate', we read written on the walls in 1968. And still today, with 40 per cent of one class of youngsters entering adult life without a job, 1992 and its starting point, the Europe of necessity, give no greater cause for dreaming – especially if the administration fails to do its job. Where are the great ideas on humanity and society?

In that respect we have never recovered the postwar climate which culminated in the 1948 Hague Congress. Some famous political personalities and many convinced activists came together then in the hope of bringing about Europe's unification and rebirth. Jean-Pierre Gouze recalls all that in his book *Les Pionniers de l'Europe Communautaire*:

Ah, how beautiful was the Europe of Europeans in that fine month of May 1948! How proudly they waved against the sky of Holland, those flags of unity proclaimed and of the ancient nations represented there. How close at hand the Europe for which they had voted so ardently seemed to so many of the delegates!

It would be easy, today, to go on about the obstacles of which this great design could not be unaware: the division of Europe, the Cold War, the pre-existence of nation-states, the ambiguous US attitude towards the construction of Europe. All that was there in outline, to be sure, but one needed to experience it.

Were our governments, apart from a few personalities and except for a few bursts of enthusiasm, preoccupied with their national problems? No doubt the first successes of Europe's construction were too slow in producing their effects. That is true, but time is needed – a great deal of time – if national interests are to be transcended, or excessively short-term views to be discarded.

The European institutions are little known, the issues are rarely explicit, public opinion in each of the twelve countries has different sensitivities, and activists in the cause of Europe are too few. In short, although the construction of Europe will have, from now on, a significant influence on our national destinies, it nevertheless remains an obscure monument or a very sophisticated adventure, known only to specialists or interest groups.

It therefore lacks the essential ingredient of our national political life: an informed, sensitive public opinion which is ready to react. In other words, unless each government and each political party does it share in explaining Europe – justifying the ideas that Europe represents, describing the various projects, explaining why certain measures have been taken and showing the advantages obtained, while also showing the concessions that have to be made – how are we to become politically effective? How, in the first place, do we obtain the desired result – that is, ensure that citizens are mobilized around what is and will be one of the fundamental issues of our future: a strong, united and influential Europe?

Europe needs politicians who have chosen to fight for it, activists who will ensure its promotion in the schools, universities and business and, ultimately, a movement of opinion.

159

It is not just a matter of explaining – though we must explain – the advantages of 'objective 1992', of a great shared economic space, in terms of material prosperity and social progress. It is more a matter of making everyone aware that he must include in his national feeling a second motherland called Europe, which widens his horizon, his opportunities for living, working and trading with others.

Then, but only then, will the momentum which has been regained in the past few years continue onward in movement and clarity. And in it France and the French will find fresh reasons for living and acting together.

Notes

2 Interdependences

1. Services linked with the development of advanced technology – research and development, services to business and all sorts of high-added-value services which use, in particular, new communication and information technology.

2. Increase in volume.

3. The La Plaza agreements of October 1986 nevertheless showed that there had been some progress towards recognizing the need for regulations covering more than the play of market forces.

4 A New Departure

1. *1992 the Challenge*, with a preface by Jacques Delors, Paris: Flammarion 1988.

6 The French in Dire Need of the State

1. Stanley Hoffmann, *Decline or Renewal? France Since the 1930s*, New York 1974, p. 446.

7 Modernizers of the Republic

1. The only exception was agriculture, where modernization really was a common objective.

2. Michel Crozier, *Etat modeste, Etat moderne*, Paris: Fayard 1987, p. 85.

3. Crozier, p. 19.

9 State and Society: Towards a New Synergy

1. See the perfectly relevant view of Andrw Schonfield on the relationship between volume and effectiveness. 'The Japanese . . . have much the smallest ratio of public expenditure of any advanced industrial country; yet there is no doubt about the effectiveness or the frequency with which government agencies intervene in the management of the Japanese economy. It is the *function* adopted by the state rather than its mass which counts'. (*In Defence of Mixed Economy*, London: Oxford Univerity Press 1984, p.4). This view is as valid in the social as in the economic sphere.

2. Here again I am borrowing ideas expressed by Jacques Donzelot.

10 The Challenge of Economic Performance

1. France is not alone in losing shares of the world market. This fate has befallen most of the countries in Europe, including Germany. On this see Michèle Debonneuil and Michel Delattre, in *Economie et Statistiques*, October 1988.

11 The Evolving Enterprise

1. The 'Fordist compromise' means exchanging wage increase for increased productivity achieved by intensfying work and reducing the worker's autonomy.

12 We Must Not Resign Ourselves to Unemployment

1. According to the OECD calculations, *Employment Prospects, 1987*. It should be recalled that in 1979 unemployment rates were already vastly different: 2.1 in Japan, 3.3 in the Federal Republic of Germany, 5.8 in the United States and 6 per cent in France.

2. J. Freyssinet, *Le Chômage*, Paris: La Découverte 1985.

3. Social data, INSEE 1987.

4. Diane Bellemare and Lise Poulin-Simon, *Le Défi du plein-emploi*, Quebec: St Martin 1983.

13 A Different Way of Living and Working

1. Alain Marc's term.

2. Cf. J.-B. de Foucauld, *La Fin du social-colbertisme*, Paris: Belfond 1988.

3. A. Bresson's term.

4. B. Preel, *Essais sur l'avenir des services*, vol. 3, Brussels: BIPE March 1986.

5. Time under constraint includes travelling to and from work, professional work and domestic work. The calculations excludes time devoted to hygiene, sleep and meals.

6. On this, see the writings of G. Roustang.

7. Confédération Française Démocratique de Travail, *Activité en friche . . . gisements d'emploi*, Paris 1987.

8. A. Hirschman, *Vers une économie politique élargie*, Paris: Editions de Minuit, 1986, pp. 31, 32.

9. Alain Touraine, *Le Modèle japonais, Japon, le consensus* (a collective work), Economica 1984.

10. BIPE forecasts.

11. According to estimates by the Centre for Employment Studies.

15   Reconstructing Employment

1. V. Merle, 'Chômage et chômeurs', *Les Temps Modernes*, November 1987.

2. R. Salais, N. Baverez and B. Reynaud, *L'Invention du chômage: histoire et transformations d'une catégorie en France, des années 1890 aux années 1980*, Paris: Presses Universitaires de France 1986.

3. O. Garnier, in *Le Travail*, INSEE–Economica 1986.

4. J.L. Ban, *Futuribles*, 1987.

5. Salais in Salais *et al.*

6. John Rawls, *A Theory of Justice*, Oxford 1972.

7. See the work done by *Echange et Projects* on the revolution of elective time (Note 11 below).

8. Employment inquiry, March 1987.

9. This is one of the differences between the Seguin Act and the Delebarre Act.

10. In this connection, retirement at a certain age ought not to be compulsory, provided that after that age pay is reduced.

11. See *Echange et projects, la révolution du temps choisi*, Paris: Albin Michel 1980, pp. 185–201.

Index

165